One Size Fits None

One Size Fits None is a must-read for anyone grappling with the systemic breakdowns that seem to define our era – whether it's crumbling infrastructure, unresponsive institutions, or the deepening climate crisis. Instead of searching for a single, scalable fix (Go Big or Go Home), the authors challenge us to rethink problem solving itself: How might we empower a generation hungry to make a change, the way Apple and Microsoft once empowered hundreds of millions through personal computing? What if we empowered local innovators to develop solutions tailored to their communities, while learning from each other in real-time? The real challenge, the book argues, is redefining who we believe has the power to innovate. Backed by original research, this book makes a compelling case that such a shift is not only possible but necessary within the decade. A revolution isn't sparked by one person alone, but by countless people experimenting, sharing, and building change together.

— ***Sebastian Groh***, **cofounder and CEO, SOLshare, Earthshot finalist, and winner, Zayed Sustainability Prize**

One Size Fits None holds the blueprint for an innovation revolution. Crawford and Plavin-Masterman argue convincingly that the biggest challenges we face today – from climate change, to disruption from technological change, to unresponsive corporations, governments, and institutions – require a completely different approach to finding solutions. The key to a better future comes from broadening who gets to innovate through developing experimentation as a mindset. Following the authors' journey over years of practical application of their methods shows that, not only will the solutions *not come* from the traditional halls of elite entrepreneurs, venture capitalists, and private equity bankers, but the solutions will be far superior when developed at the local level by those who are most familiar with the problems at hand and arrive, through experimentation, at outcomes that would benefit them directly.

— ***Michael Horvath***, **economist and cofounder, Strava**

One Size Fits None strips away the hype of AI, algorithms, and Big Tech invincibility, and confirms their real effects on our lives – then shows us a better way. Yes, technology can seem able to do anything for us, not only help us buy or stream anything we want with one click, but also serve all our lifestyle desires. While tech visionaries rhapsodize about it as companion, babysitter, teacher, and co-author, we've all become part of a "cattle class" struggling to get the help we need because it isn't one of the menu options. *One Size Fits None* reminds us that the better way is human ingenuity; data shows that real people can develop real solutions that actually work – for us. This brilliant book will make you feel seen, and inspire you to take back the initiative and seek solutions among the wildly diverse, messy miracles of humanity itself.

— ***Barclay Palmer***, **executive editor, *Climate and Capital Media***

We've all been victimized by the "doom loop," where no well-informed human can ever answer our urgent questions about our bills, our 103 degree fever, our blue-screen computer, the climate crisis, you name it. *One Size Fits None* explains how we got here, how much damage these loops are causing, and – most importantly – how we can escape them. The simple solution, the authors argue, is to scale down our businesses and unleash millions of small-scale enterprises capable of delivering personalized and localized goods and services. They persuasively show that we have the right tools – of design, ingenuity, and capital – to create these kinds of solutions, if we're smart enough to use them. And there's no better book to explain what these tools should be, and no better time to deploy them than now.

— ***Michael Shuman*, publisher, *Main Street Journal***

One Size Fits None: Time for an Entrepreneurial Revolution

BY

ALEJANDRO JUÁREZ CRAWFORD

Democratizing Innovation Institute, USA

AND

MIRIAM PLAVIN-MASTERMAN

Worcester State University, USA

emerald
PUBLISHING

United Kingdom – North America – Japan – India – Malaysia – China

Emerald Publishing Limited
Emerald Publishing, Floor 5, Northspring, 21-23 Wellington Street, Leeds LS1 4DL

First edition 2025

Reprints and permissions service
Contact: www.copyright.com

British Library Cataloguing in Publication Data
A catalogue record for this book is available from the British Library

ISBN: 978-1-83608-663-5 (Print)
ISBN: 978-1-83608-660-4 (Online)
ISBN: 978-1-83608-662-8 (Epub)

INVESTOR IN PEOPLE

Contents

About the Authors

Alejandro Juárez Crawford, as cofounder of the Democratizing Innovation Institute and cocreator of the RebelBase platform, leads a global collaboration enabling people to build solutions of their own. He serves as clinical professor of innovation at the Bard MBA in Sustainability and cohosts the *What if Instead?* podcast with Miriam.

Miriam Plavin-Masterman is a Professor in the Business Administration/ Economics department at Worcester State University. She studies how social entrepreneurs repurpose industrial infrastructure to make cities more livable. She cohosts the *What if Instead?* podcast with Alejandro.

Acknowledgments

This book began as we grappled with a series of questions. Why can't we fight climate change? Why am I stuck in a doom loop? Could these things be related?

We asked ourselves these questions while working on a series of op-eds with the cleantech investor and *Climate and Capital* executive editor Barclay Palmer, who pushed us to articulate the underlying question more clearly. We are grateful for his insights at the start of this process.

Fiona Allison, our editor at Emerald Publishing, went above and beyond what we could hope for in an editor. We're incredibly lucky to have her as a thoughtful (and good-humored) champion of our work and an overall force for good in the world.

We thank the members of the Emerald production team for their talent and hard work in putting this together.

We deeply appreciate Larry Koffler, Kristina Kohl, Hunter Lovins, Frederico Menino, Bob Osborne, and Moose Shuman for invaluable feedback and advice.

We're grateful to our parents, David and Adrienne Plavin, Richard Crawford, and Milika Nevárez, for reading drafts, raising troublemakers, making tea, playing music, and taking the crucial photo in the clutch, and to Nevaris and the late Steve Crawford, for believing in you while never letting you get away with anything.

Last but certainly not least, when in doubt, ask Chris and Tuba what they think. We can't possibly express how much we appreciate the ongoing lesson in what it means to surround yourself with those who love you most and criticize you best.

Please Listen Carefully, as Our Options Have Recently Changed

Increasingly, we live and work in one-size-fits-none systems. When you hear the phrase "your needs are very important to us," you know you are lost in one of these systems. It is magical thinking to believe they will suddenly become responsive – even to address the biggest crises of our time. Time for a new plan.

People – perhaps especially young people – know they have inherited a bad bargain (Flynn, 2021). As unresponsive models lock up markets and governments, escaping life in cattle class increasingly means working for organizations that perpetuate it. If you are young today, you are competing for roles within sputtering models that will not even begin to meet human needs in the years to come. This vicious cycle rewards rising talent for signing on to spread unresponsive systems. To hope such systems will evolve into responsive ones is naive at best. When we look to corporate promises or annual "conference of the parties" (COP) events to restore responsiveness, we are like Charlie Brown, trying once more to kick the football, only to have it pulled away again (Roman, 1981).

Most of us have answers, when asked what should just work differently. Here in the doom loop, we can imagine solutions that better meet our needs. Perhaps more surprisingly, many of us relish the chance to work on one of those solutions. The closing section of this book presents powerful new research showing how we come to life when given space to try. When we ask "what if instead?" and respond with experiments of our own – or even just help others with their experiments – we emerge more capable of conducting such experiments.

The evidence for this is powerful. It points to an opening that's ours to miss. However unresponsive the digital age has become, we can open up spaces and improve platforms for people everywhere to build alternatives. Instead of hoping that today's systems might be made responsive, we can use the technologies that now divide us to connect us in building solutions that respond to our needs. Time to launch an entrepreneurial revolution.

***

What does trying to reach your bank on the phone have to do with the oil industry celebrating at a global climate conference?

One Size Fits None, 1–3

Copyright © 2025 Alejandro Juárez Crawford and Miriam Plavin-Masterman

Published under exclusive licence by Emerald Publishing Limited

doi:10.1108/978-1-83608-660-420251001

The systems organizing our lives feel increasingly out of touch, even when they work as designed. Scalable systems serve many people, at little or no additional cost for each person served. Such systems can be great investments. They can also become increasingly *unresponsive*. When you hit a glitch in the system – a flight delay or a problem with your luggage – you have no recourse. Do you fight valiantly to reach someone who might understand your needs and try to help? More likely, you get an automated response, which impressively recycles the language of sympathy for your situation. Salt on a wound? This is the system working as designed.

Air travel is hardly the only place where we encounter this, but it aptly illustrates "life in cattle class." If you thought cattle class was bad now, wait until all you can do is complain to the Artificial Intelligence (AI) agent, while the systems around you become ever less responsive.

Did you ever have a friend, a family member, or someone you worked with, who used the same responses in every situation – or tried to vary them so they seemed plausibly appropriate while investing as little attention as possible? When your bank, your hospital, your service provider, or your government does this, it's no accident. In fact, for those squeezing responsiveness from the system, the fact that you *cannot* get anyone to address your needs is a feature, not a bug.

You still patronize the business, public agency, or community program, which is now cheaper to operate. Private firms and government agencies race to outdo each other in pursuit of this goal, variously called efficiency, scalability, optimization, or flywheel effects. Capital chases the returns such efficiency and scalability promise. When the systems in which you live and work dispense with your needs as cheaply as possible, it produces life in cattle class. The cheap seats on an airplane or ship are a shorthand for systems that squeeze life ever tighter, everywhere except in the premium seats.

Unresponsive models efficiently handle the most common situations, but they're often too efficient to work when the chips are down. These models now surround us from the earliest age, and not just when we fly. If and when you finally reach a real person at the bank, telecom provider, or government office, that person often struggles to get the system to help with anything but a few predefined needs. Examples pepper daily life, wherever you need something not "on the menu." A relative of one of the authors recently tried to respond to check fraud and identity theft. He called his bank over and over, spending an entire week in the communications "doom loop" many of us know so well. Finally, he went into his bank and explained the situation. The people at the bank tried to be helpful. *They couldn't make the system work either.*

When responsive systems become luxuries, most of us are a little closer to a crisis. Sometimes, consequences are trivial, and the greatest cost is frustration. In other cases, the hit can be significant – to your physical or financial health, or the health of your company, community, or natural environment. The doctor soaks your implant in a drug to which you are allergic – and when you note this right before going under anesthesia, asks you, "How allergic are you?" Mid-flight, the panels fall off the side of your plane (Surowiecki, 2024). Such examples sound almost comical. They blanket everyday life.

When attention to the details of our circumstances becomes a luxury, no wonder we get no action on larger crises. Unresponsive systems worsen local crises and keep us from addressing the global climate crisis. These trends may seem separate. They're not.

The spread of unresponsive systems blunts our capacity to respond to disasters. It also hamstrings our ability to address their causes. As the 2025 wildfires engulfed Los Angeles, well over half its fire trucks were out of service. Turns out, fire truck prices, replacement parts prices, and production times had skyrocketed after a private equity "rollup" consolidated production (Musharbash, 2025). No jurisdiction or industry has a monopoly on unresponsiveness. When fires spread across southern Turkey in 2021, it came out that the country had built a fraction of planned fire-responder aircraft and safety roads (Butler, 2021), while senior government officials stood accused of plundering public coffers.

Unresponsiveness seems cheap, even smart, when fair winds blow, but could not cost more. A longtime firefighter who has personally faced down some of the worst fires in her state's history recently wrote: "Unless we implement the climate solutions we have that are now cheaper than continuing to burn fossil energy, nowhere will be safe from climate catastrophe" (Lovins, 2025). Each year, as storms and wildfires spread, industry and government leaders convene from around the world. They come out with a joint acknowledgment that something is happening, and something probably should be done about it (UNFCCC, 2023). Might as well just say they "value you as a customer," while you wait on hold.

Part I

The Real Cost of the Hockey Stick

> All through my life I've had this strange unaccountable feeling that something was going on in the world, something big, even sinister, and no one would tell me what it was. – *The Hitchhiker's Guide to the Galaxy* (Adams, 1979, p. 199)

Chapter 1

No Recourse

That's a Different Department

In January 2025, Dr. Elisabeth Potter was in the operating room (OR) to conduct a breast reconstruction procedure for a cancer patient. The patient was already under anesthesia when, Dr. Potter recounts, she "got a phone call into the OR saying that UnitedHealthcare wanted me to call them about one of the patients who was having surgery today – who was actually asleep on the operating table – and you know, said I had to call right now" (Potter, 2025).

So she left the OR (with another surgeon still there) and called UnitedHealthcare (UHC). "A gentleman said he needed some information . . . wanted to know her diagnosis and whether her in-patient stay could be justified." Potter recalls asking, in response, "Do you understand she's asleep [that is, anesthetized] right now and she has breast cancer? And the gentleman said 'Actually I don't. That's a different department that would know that information'" (Potter, 2025).

The man on the phone couldn't respond to the situation at hand – not even after the surgeon explained that she had a patient under anesthesia for cancer-related breast surgery. No matter the view from the OR, the doctor's circumstances, not to mention those of her patient, didn't fit the model. Potter concludes: "I was like: 'Well, she does need to stay overnight. . . . And you have all the information . . . because I got approval for this surgery. And I need to go back and be with my patient now'" (Potter, 2025).[1]

The unresponsive system ensures you know your place when you try to get someone to respond to your specific situation. When the agent says, "That's a different department," the next sentence, though seldom said aloud, is right there between the lines. "And if you have a problem with this, well, what are you gonna do about it?"

---

[1]UHC denied the cancer patient's overnight stay. Then, in February 2025, defamation lawyers representing UHC sent Dr. Potter a letter insisting that "UnitedHealthcare never asked or expected you to step out of surgery," and demanding: "You must promptly correct the record by removing your videos, posting a public apology to UnitedHealthcare. . . ." The doctor posted the letter on Instagram (Potter, 2025).

One Size Fits None, 7–15
Copyright © 2025 Alejandro Juárez Crawford and Miriam Plavin-Masterman
Published under exclusive licence by Emerald Publishing Limited
doi:10.1108/978-1-83608-660-420251002

These are the words of the person who has given you a raw deal, and knows you know it, but also knows you have no recourse. They're the words of the person who knows you have to settle for what they offer, however many times the scripted statement insists "our customers are valuable to us" (cue endless hold music).

And what *are* you gonna do about it? Scream at the person on the other end of the phone? He probably works at a call center, where he must follow rules and procedures designed to contain costs. As AI agents perform more of his job, they too will respond as algorithms dictate.

What are you gonna do about it when the unresponsiveness impacts your industry or your community? What will you do when it disrupts vital natural systems? Go door to door signing folks up for a class action lawsuit, as in a movie? Do you have years to wait for a small check? Today, while you try to get your bank, your internet, or your healthcare to work, natural catastrophes and extreme heat encumber daily life for more and more of us. The planet, like the cancer patient, needs attention now. Our systems aren't set up to respond.

All over the world, the climate crisis makes its presence known. Many of us have now experienced increasingly frequent hurricanes, floods, and wildfires, deteriorating agricultural conditions, and dysfunctional government responses. "Among the 20,000 respondents surveyed by Deloitte across 20 countries in September 2024, 56% have personally experienced at least one climate-linked extreme weather event within the last six months" (Steinmann et al., 2025). Others may identify with those who have lived through these conditions – or worry about the next generation.

What are you gonna do about *that?*

The crisis appears in everything from asthma rates, through property insurability, to toxic chemical levels near major cities. We read the latest story about a historic heat wave, dying bees, constant storms, rising floodwaters, and unbreathable air from wildfires. Tens of millions of people already flee extreme weather events. The Institute for Economics and Peace projects that hundreds of millions will flee as the climate crisis advances (McAllister, 2024). Unless we change course dramatically, survivable temperatures, fresh water, and sufficient nutrition will become luxuries inaccessible to many.

When it comes to the climate disaster, most people see the iceberg ahead – especially in the generations that bear its worst consequences. When the UNDP conducted the largest-ever survey of public opinion on climate change in 2021, nearly 70% of those under 18 flagged climate change as a global emergency (Poushter et al., 2022). A further 2021 study of 10,000 youth from 10 countries found that over 50% of young people felt sad, anxious, angry, powerless, helpless, and guilty about climate change, while 45% said their feelings negatively affected their daily lives. Countries with higher levels of concern tended to be poorer, often in the Global South, or if in the Global North, to have been directly affected by climate change (Flynn, 2021).

Technical options for addressing this abound. Replacements for the fossil economy are proven and practical. Commercializing their use could create waves of jobs. To remake every industry to run without fossil fuels might be the economic opportunity of the century. But that opportunity threatens some of the most powerful firms in the world, which would see their lucrative products and business models disrupted into irrelevance.

Those incumbents currently have their hands in your pocket, using your tax dollars to keep their failing models operating. They maintain the fiction that their businesses are highly competitive, while they depend on subsidies so massive that these subsidies constitute a significant portion of total global economic output.

Your Tax Dollars at Work

Take away the subsidies that keep fossil fuels on life support, and they barely compete. We can't know what innovators might develop in the absence of subsidies for incumbents. What we know for sure is that these incumbents fail to compete on their merits right now. If the global economy were a twelve-slice pizza, fossil fuel subsidies alone would make up a small slice. According to the International Monetary Fund, "globally, fossil fuel subsidies were $7 trillion in 2022 or 7.1 percent of GDP" (Black et al., 2023). Your tax dollars at work. These handouts that keep obsolete industries running grow with each global climate conference and every green marketing campaign.

Talk about an unresponsive system. While people everywhere watch fires burn and storms rage, and many go to great lengths to try and improve their behavior within the system, we continue to sink a major portion of global economic output into artificially propping up fossil fuels. As companies and governments issue statements about tapering down gradually over *decades,* it can feel as if those subsidies are locked in place.

Where do you turn for recourse? Large institutional investors? The governments of the leading economies? Early-stage venture firms, with their capacity to seed something better, in theory? All of the above?

Changing these institutions can sound like a fool's errand. They're already unresponsive to most of the people who use them every day. Please listen carefully, as our options have recently changed. Press 1 if you fit one of the limited situations our script can handle. Better yet, chat with our bot, or our "AI agent."

We're Experiencing Some Turbulence

Despite rising climate anxiety, the exposure of much of the world's population to the ravages of climate change can seem like so much data. On an unseasonably pleasant winter's day in a city in the Global North, climate catastrophe can feel rather abstract. In the meantime, we carry on using the systems we've got. Take flying, for example (speaking of cattle class). With about 10% of the population flying each year, air travel accounts for 2.5% of global emissions. Since 1990, air freight has roughly quadrupled, and air travel has tripled (Ritchie, 2024). The carbon intensity of air travel has not improved in the meantime. Fuel efficiency has improved, but increasing air travel and air freight far outweigh these gains. By 2023, annual emissions from aviation passed a billion tons and continue to rise steadily (Ritchie, 2024).

Fun fact: as air travel changes the climate, the changing climate changes air travel too. "Recent research indicates that [air] turbulence is rising and that climate change is a cause, specifically, elevated carbon dioxide emissions that affect air currents" (Moses & Suhartono, 2024). Anyone who's felt their stomach drop when a flight lurched abruptly has heard the reassuring voice over the loudspeaker, telling us the turbulence will be temporary. Turns out, as we continue to spew carbon, such disturbances become more frequent.

As chaos crops up everywhere, each faction and social group knows there's someone to blame. But if you look carefully at the picture, a seductive way of meeting human needs and a certain class of problem solver can be seen lurking at the edge of the frame.

Ever notice how the options seem to change in lockstep for many services? Suddenly all the providers make you pay for something that used to be free. You have the illusion of choice. Perhaps it's not as bad as waiting in line for government-rationed goods, but the two experiences have more in common than we might admit. You *have no recourse*, whether you're trying to get the tax man to fix an error or learning that your local hospital got consolidated with others in your city or region, and now lacks a basic capability it's always had (Nocera & McLean, 2023).

In one country, decent healthcare becomes a luxury. In another, healthcare remains widely accessible, but buildings are built to collapse during that country's earthquakes. What if we stop talking about these as isolated cases, and look at the broader trends that make investing in unresponsive systems so profitable – and life in cattle class increasingly normal? Whether it's a cell phone plan or a baggage charge, when markets become consolidated, and dominated by a few large providers, these providers have little incentive to perform. Eventually, consumers and workers line up and take what's on offer.

Unresponsive systems work in the base case – and seem to be cheap or free while the base case holds. This can be seductive, especially when you can barely afford housing, healthcare, debt payments, transportation, or the technology critical for work and social life. So consumers sign on to unresponsive systems. Consider your recent experiences dealing with a digital device (or a company on the phone). Has there been a moment when you were subtly "invited" into cattle class? Talk to a doctor on telehealth! Click here to be connected to our AI Agent, our "live" chat! It's the fastest option! You get something out of this. What have you signed away?

It Looked Like Such a Bargain

Most of us cannot resist. Companies design systems to be sensitive to our preferences and responsive to our needs – up until we opt in. After that, we're cheap or free to serve. Extensive investment is justified to exploit our weaknesses since few of us will deal with the headache of opting out later. No matter how frustrated we become once we've signed on, we'll take the bait.

Cheap has also come to dominate many business decisions, like Boeing outsourcing engineering or your local hospital getting bought up by a private equity firm. In both cases, someone determined that cutting costs would generate outsized profits. This makes a few people a lot of money, until your doctor gets evaluated on how fast she can treat the most patients, or the merger that sold off Boeing's engineering excellence cracks under the strain of treating building planes like a finance business. This only makes the news when things come to a head – when panels fall off a plane. All the while, businesses and governments automate the options as far as we let them. Of course, life in cattle class comes with a "premium" alternative, but wait until you see the price for *that.*

For generations now, business school students have been taught to look at businesses less in terms of making things work well over time and more as optimization problems. Managers learn to build models that cut costs, "monetize" premium options, and lock up markets. Do not underestimate the decisions they drive with spreadsheets showing short-term wins. This goes beyond profit-seeking organizations, as public and social sector organizations strive to serve as many people as possible as cheaply as possible.

Nothing wrong with efficiency, until it dominates caring for patients or building planes. A company loses focus on such details as it pursues maximum returns for shareholders in the next quarter. A school gets a 3-D printer or a set of tablet computers with no accounting for required upgrades and supplies. Take our systems, and wring the responsiveness out. But how good is cheap when a surgeon is being called out of the OR to justify the cost?

Responsiveness becomes a *luxury*, an opportunity for premium pricing (Schwerin, 2022). Affordable food gets processed, "farm to table" becomes a nice-to-have, and disease rates soar. Even the simply tolerable lies squarely in the luxury zone.

You've Earned Elite Status

The more extreme the divide, the harder many of us strive to get into the premium seats, instead of changing the model. After all, who doesn't want to ski when there's no natural snow, and enjoy the out-of-season oranges, when they're right there on the shelf? If you can afford *that,* you're already in the elite group whose investing activities dwarf the carbon footprint of everyone in cattle class. At that point, it takes imagination to conjure the person who works in 110-degree heat or flees the flood or drought.

Do alternatives to this seem far out of reach? Everyday life in the not-too-distant past featured many of them. Small community banks, for example, provided personalized service and made capital available to small businesses in each region. Other alternatives abound in the minds of people who, given the chance to try out ways things could work differently, rise to the challenge. Ask a young person today what's broken, and what should just work differently, and see how many answers you get.

In Part III of this book, we'll explore the power of Apple cofounder Steve Jobs' idea that asking what should work differently is "the most important thing." Jobs spoke of "one simple fact" that "everything around you was made up by people no smarter than you. And you can change it, you can influence it, you can ... build your own things that other people can use" (Santa Clara Valley Historical Society, 1994a). We'll present original research suggesting that the readiness to do what Jobs describes is more common than it might seem.

Solving today's problems means changing whom we ask. As SOLshare founder and internationally recognized renewable energy innovator Sebastian Groh observes: "If you're exposed to something every day,... then you have a good understanding what this problem is. And if these people are empowered, I think then we [can] get good fixes" (Crawford & Plavin-Masterman, 2024b).

If you're someone with the means to avoid what's cheapest, think about how few can access what seems basic to you. A doctor who takes time and listens to you. Fresh food, free of extensive processing. A home within 30 minutes of a town center. Temperatures that won't give you heatstroke. Water that doesn't give you cancer. Air you can breathe without taking your life in your hands. Clothing that doesn't enslave kids to make. Financial services that aren't debt traps. Media that doesn't treat you like an addict to exploit. If you can choose, you've probably purchased at least one of these as a luxury or specialty item.

Life's Little Indignities

Life in cattle class leaves many of us with the persistent sensation that our experiences, our communities, and our needs are an afterthought. When the system you are dealing with cannot respond to you, you want to curse or tear your hair out. Or you acclimate pretty well, but notice an undercurrent of frustration, which comes out when there is someone to blame – another driver, the call center operator, the interloper. This applies to micro crises (no option for you on the menu of your doctor/bank/car rental/other service provider) and macro crises (wildfires have turned the sky dark and made the air unsafe to breathe).

Think about what you do to exempt yourself from these crises. Micro: the credit card you got so you could avoid the long lines or have some peace in an airport lounge; the lawyer you hired to help with financial, healthcare, or real estate issues. Macro: the clean water, air conditioning, refrigeration, and medical access you enjoy because you do not live in the Global South – or because you live in a wealthy enclave there; the plans you're making to help ensure your parents get a decent retirement; everything you'd do to get your kids into some program or activity that gives them a shot at the shrinking opportunities to avoid life in cattle class.

To say that systems have become unresponsive does not ignore material progress. In aggregate, we're richer and safer than at any point on record, which can make the malaise of dealing with an unresponsive system hard to put your finger on. That doesn't keep grievance from building under the surface as cattle class expands. Unresponsive systems feel out of touch with us and what we really want. The more unresponsive systems are, the harder we work to escape them. The more those with resources escape them, the more unresponsive systems become. That's the vicious cycle.

When will your needs become the edge case, to which the system isn't built to respond? Consider a few illustrations.

Not an option: In 2024, one of the authors' fathers was trying to extend a car rental after a car accident. When he called the main car rental company number, he was asked for his insurance policy number. When he entered it, the automated message directed him to call the local branch of the rental car company to extend his rental. So he looked up the branch's phone number and called it, which sent him back to the original number he called, and he was directed through the same process with the same recorded instructions.

He went through this process four more times with distinct starting phone numbers before finding a person who manually connected him to what was supposedly the branch number. The rental car company would not give him that direct number, and the answering machine message did not identify itself as a rental car branch. So he went in person to the branch and waited in line for over an hour. When he finally got to speak to a person at the branch, that person told him he could have extended the rental car over the phone had he pressed "5" – which was not a directory option!

Our systems do not recognize your entry: In 2019, one of the authors was dealing with a torn knee ligament, surgery, and follow-up. Her last name sometimes appears hyphenated, sometimes not, in various databases. She began receiving bills in the tens of thousands of dollars from her orthopedist, claiming she lacked coverage because her insurance company had no record of her. So she filled out the paperwork with her insurance information and sent it back to the orthopedist's billing office. When this happened again a few weeks later, she called her insurance company, quite upset, and was told that her name was being submitted incorrectly by the doctor's office. The insurance company *knew these were her claims,* but according to their processes, could only take her legal, hyphenated last name in processing them. That's an unresponsive system.

She called the orthopedist's billing department and conveyed the information the insurance company provided her, receiving assurances this would all get fixed quickly. Two weeks later, she got the orthopedist's paperwork asking for thousands of dollars a third time, and threatening to send her unpaid bill to a collections agency. At that point, she tried a different approach. She stapled copies of her insurance card to the paperwork and added a note saying "I spoke to my insurance company and they said you are not submitting my name correctly. Billing already knows this. Do your job!" She finally got a phone call from the orthopedist's billing office, in which they apologized and explained that their bill submission systems could not handle hyphenated last names, so they had needed to call her insurance company and speak directly to someone to get the claims processed.

We cannot fix our mistake: In 2024, a family in Nottinghamshire, England, found out that the local registrar had incorrectly marked their new baby girl Lilah's sex as male on her official birth certificate. They were given apologies by the registrar and the area manager, then told by the "General Register Office (GRO)..., responsible for administering all civil registration in England and Wales, and the Home Office ... that Lilah's birth certificate cannot be reissued, although an amendment can be made in the margin of the original document.... There is currently no facility in law that allows for correct certificates to be issued that show the correct information only, without reproduction of the marginal note." The Home Office also confirmed that there was no flexibility under the law (Hill, 2024).

In these cases, unresponsive systems externalize, or push, the cost of their unresponsiveness onto those using them.[2] With the car rental, the cost consisted of multiple phone calls, travel time, and an in-person visit. For the torn ligament, it added up to a few months of stress, paperwork, and multiple phone calls. For the Nottinghamshire family, it portends a potential doom loop. How many times will they have to try and get someone to read a marginal note on their daughter's birth certificate – when she signs up for school, applies for a passport or driver's license, or tries to play a sport?

The Only Game in Town

You have no recourse because alternatives have been systematically eliminated. If there is an industry or government program where unresponsive models have not yet taken over, look for mergers and acquisitions or large consulting contracts on the horizon.

Let's start with the travel industry since we've drawn the term cattle class from it. Behind today's nightmares lie decades of consolidation. The number of airlines has dwindled. The largest now share institutional owners. In Europe, cross-country mergers include Air France/KLM (pursuing a stake in SAS at the time of writing), Lufthansa/ITA, and IAG (British Airways' and Iberia's parent company), to name a few. In the United States, as Pat Garofalo notes in his Boondoggle blog, "Since the 1970s, dozens of airlines have consolidated down to just a handful. Delta, for example, is the result of 16 different mergers. American is the result of 12, United is 7 and Southwest is 5. Making matters worse, the four biggest [U.S.] airlines are all partially owned by the same common, dominant institutional investors" (Garofalo, 2024).

This consolidation translates directly into the misery of life in cattle class, including "new lows in customer service, increasingly opaque pricing, and worse

---

[2]An externality is a consequence of an activity not reflected in that activity's cost, and not primarily borne by those directly involved in the activity.

labor conditions, none of which has prevented the industry from needing to be bailed out by the public repeatedly, even as large parts of the country see reduced service or lose service altogether" (Garofalo, 2024). Rental cars, trains, hotels, and booking services have been consolidated, too. The travel industry has been just one target of this effort, Garofalo notes: "Overall, in the last 30 years, 75 percent of US industries have grown more consolidated, with that marked drop in choice leading to worse customer service and labor conditions, as well as higher prices" (Garofalo, 2024).

While in some cases the United States has led the consolidation charge, the conquest has been global. According to a 2021 analysis by the McKinsey Global Institute of the growing "share of overall economic activity attributable to large corporations ... over the past 25 years, the relative weight of large corporations has increased." "By 2018, [their] share had risen to almost 30 percent of home-country GDP on average, about a 60 percent rise [over 1995 levels]..." (Manyika et al., 2021, p. 14).

There's nothing inevitable about such consolidation. For 50 years, top finance and consulting firms have hungrily and systematically sought out industries to which to apply their models. In later chapters, we'll explore these models' mechanics. We'll delve into how one-size-fits-none models came to be so pervasive over the last 50 years of human civilization. We'll also present an alternative – one that lies close at hand, ready to be seized – and what happens if we fail.

Here's the kicker – these systems remain unresponsive to crises ranging from the customer service doom loop to the warming of the planet to irreversible levels. Collect billions in taxpayer money while failing to respond to small businesses trying to get pandemic relief and stiffing the accountants and others who signed on to help? That's what a raft of class action lawsuits allege. Make billions from financing new fossil fuel exploration when the scientific consensus says we can afford none? "The purpose of a system is what it does" (Beer, 2002, p. 217). Some of the same banks alleged to have been unresponsive to the needs of everyday customers during the pandemic have, since 2017, committed $7 trillion to finance fossil fuels (not to be confused with the trillions in global subsidies each year). As of 2024, JPMorgan Chase and Citigroup together had committed more than $800 billion, with Citigroup taking the lead in financing new extraction projects (Shraiman et al., 2024). Large global banks finance the fossil *future* at a time when 40% of human beings list climate as our top concern, according to APCO's 2023 surveys of tens of thousands of people in 39 countries (APCO, 2023).

This requires no conspiracy. As we lay out in Part II, it reflects a paradigm we train and reward consultants, bankers, investors, and others to spread across industries. But it is far from hopeless. As we show in Part III, we face an unprecedented opportunity to create new, responsive systems now.

Chapter 2

Business Class Ticket Holders May Now Begin Boarding

The Lion's Share of Emissions

Despite the hoopla around green investments, emissions continue at untenable levels. Why?

Maybe you're trying to compost your kitchen waste or avoid buying clothing or electronics designed to be quickly replaced. Or maybe you're tired of high gas prices when you need affordable fuel to get to work or heat your home. In the first case, maybe you can't understand people driving giant, new, gas-guzzling vehicles, wearing fast fashion, or eating factory-farmed meat. In the second case, maybe you've had it with the superior attitude of people wearing their Patagonia vests and bringing their own cups to Starbucks in their shiny electric vehicles (EVs).

Both perspectives probably miss the point. Intensive efforts to reduce personal carbon footprints win battles but are losing the war. Since 1990, "emissions from low-and middle-income groups within rich countries declined" (Chancel, 2022). But this hasn't made a dent, because for the top 1%, per capita emissions have *increased* in the same period. Since 1990, the poorer half "of the world population has been responsible for only 16% of all emissions growth." By contrast, "the top 1% has been responsible for 23% of the total" (Chancel, 2022).

Some ultra-wealthy people enjoy carbon-intensive lifestyles, but that's not what's responsible for the problem. Instead, it's the systems in which they invest. For top emitters, the lion's share of emissions derives from investment, not consumption. According to Oxfam, the investing activities of the world's 125 wealthiest individuals each emit an average of *3 million* tons of carbon annually. That's a million times the *3 tons* the average person in the *bottom 90%* emits (Maitland et al., 2022).

The unresponsive systems underwritten by the investments of a few determine the carbon the rest of us will emit (or inhale) just trying to live our lives. Emissions driven by the investments of the richest 1% are projected to cause 1.3 million heat-related deaths between 2020 and 2030, roughly the entire population of Dallas, Texas (Oxfam, 2023). That only counts deaths directly from heat.

One Size Fits None, 17–22

Copyright © 2025 Alejandro Juárez Crawford and Miriam Plavin-Masterman
Published under exclusive licence by Emerald Publishing Limited
doi:10.1108/978-1-83608-660-420251003

Greenhouse Gas Emissions vs.   Income Brackets
Income Bracket

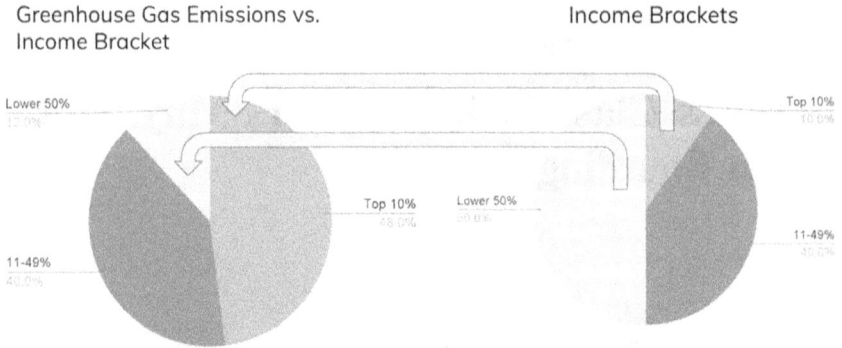

Fig. 1.   Percent of Annual per Capita GHG Emissions vs. Income
Distribution Percent. *Source:* Adapted from Chancel (2022).

This goes beyond just a few individuals, however. When you include investing activities, 10% of people do nearly half the damage, while fully half of us generate just over 10% (More precisely, 50% do 12%, while 10% do 48% (Chancel, 2022), as shown in Fig. 1.) That's like a party where one person generates half the dirty dishes, while half the guests share a single plate.

The rest of us can adopt carbon-conscious options until the end of time, but it won't do the job unless we participate in building new, far more responsive systems.

However much you might hear about ESG – investing that incorporates environmental, social, or governance goals – the numbers tell a simple story. Investing activity has doubled down on fossil fuels (Chancel, 2022).

If you are tempted to conclude "case closed – a few rich people are to blame," read on. This game wants your participation.

Blame the Game, Not the Player

Aspirational careers, in finance, consulting, technology, and management, support the spread of one-size-fits-none models. And many of the most attractive investment opportunities lie in expanding those models. If that's the game on offer, we're not sure it does much good for individuals to refuse to play it. Using your attractive salary to fund a perfectly green life won't change things either. Nor will joining a small-scale food coop, becoming vegan, or consuming only regeneratively raised beef, for that matter. Nor will biking to work or driving an EV. Nor will abandoning fast fashion and wearing and repairing a few, high-quality garments. Individual efforts to reduce your carbon footprint send a market signal, which gets drowned out by interference. Part II of this book describes how this interference works and why it matters.

All of these individual practices and others have value, but they won't be enough unless we take part in replacing the way we do things today. That doesn't mean everyone must become an innovator or entrepreneur, the way we typically think of one. People can lend their skills, their resources, and their access to everyday experiments to replace the fossil economy throughout their industries and communities. To do so proves far more practical and contagious than it might sound, as we detail in Part III. We won't get there through top-down planning. It's time to stop believing that we can take systems not designed to respond to the concerns of the everyday people who use them, and can nudge those systems in the right direction.

Headlong Into the Abyss

The world's biggest capital providers, including big banks and governments, continue with business as usual. We have mentioned global subsidies and the role of leading banks; this involves more than a few bad actors. From 2015 to 2022, according to Forbes, "the world's 60 largest private banks financed fossil fuels with $6.9 trillion. Nearly half – $3.3 trillion – went towards fossil fuel expansion, despite the acknowledgment from the International Energy Agency that there was no room for new fossil fuels if we are to achieve net zero by 2050." In 2023 alone, banks financed $705 billion in fossil fuels, half for fossil fuel *expansion* (Jackson, 2024).

For the first time, in 2024, average global temperatures *passed* the internationally recognized red alert threshold of 1.5°C above preindustrial levels (Borenstein, 2025). At that level, we're already seeing extraordinary impact. A 2024 report commissioned by the International Chamber of Commerce pinpoints almost 4,000 extreme weather events that impacted 1.6 billion people from 2014 to 2023 and cost the world $2 trillion in direct and indirect damage (International Chamber of Commerce, 2024). If those sound like so many numbers, think of a news story about a recent wildfire, flood, or heat wave that affected someone you know, and then consider that the same thing is happening elsewhere, or will happen again somewhere soon. Climate change poses the most significant worldwide threat to human health (Atwoli et al., 2021).

We're already there. We're set to produce more than double the fossil fuels in 2030 than the 1.5° threshold would allow (SEI, 2023). Governments project their economies in the 2020s to produce 460% more coal, 83% more gas, and 29% more oil each year than would allow the world to remain at the threshold (Anderson, 2023). That's if countries around the world were to stick to planned emissions, which they have yet to do.

When you look at *actual* trends instead of planned emissions, the picture gets much worse. The World Health Organization (WHO) highlights the risks climate change poses to breathable air, safe drinking water, nutritious food, and safe shelter. Their 2022 report projects that between 2030 and 2050, climate change will cause about 250,000 additional yearly deaths from malnutrition, malaria, dengue, diarrhea, and heat stress (World Health Organization, 2022).

As bad as it gets if we head in the current direction, it does not have to end up that way. People everywhere have what it takes to find new ways to meet our needs in abundance. But it is hard to conduct new experiments when we are breathlessly running to escape from cattle class.

Get Out While You Can

For those who can afford it, the escape industry is booming. Take travel: "If you go to upscale, you're actually seeing growth there," said Adam Sacks, the president of tourism economics at Oxford Economics (Smialek, 2024). While the escapes of the wealthy command attention, it's not just them. If you're enjoying a pleasant day in a northern climate as you read this, remember that those squeezing the responsiveness out of our systems need you to keep reaching to achieve a decent life. They need you stretched far too thin to think about building more responsive ones. They depend on you dedicating your talent and resources to their systems.

Perhaps you accept cattle class in one part of your life, so you can escape it in another – or can help your children to do so. You sacrifice to get your kids into the best schools, or a chance to study in a global center. Or you work your tail off in a rich country to bring your kids there, one by one (coyotes are not cheap).[1] Or you fight tooth and nail to keep out migrants you see as competing for scarce opportunities and taking your spot.

Some forms of refuge from cattle class are more mundane. You work in an air-conditioned office. You vacation somewhere pristine. Maybe you dream of moving to a "climate haven" (only for floods or fires to reach there, too) (Teirstein, 2024). Meanwhile, you get what you need to be delivered, knowing, somewhere in the back of your mind, that someone labored in the restaurant kitchen, mined the minerals for the device battery, or stitched the clothes in the box.

If air conditioning or living in the Global North seems trivial or simply normal, consider this. While writing this book, one of the authors taught a course in collaboration with Dr. Kate O'Neill, then dean of the College of Business at the American University in Baghdad. They held calls on days when the temperature exceeded 120 degrees Fahrenheit in Iraq, dropping to 112 or 113 at night. On one call, O'Neill explained that fire alarms rang in the background because the heat caused chemicals to combust – a regular occurrence (O'Neill, 2024). Globally, July 2024 recorded the hottest day up to that point in recorded history (Niranjan, 2024).

As the heat intensifies, workers in vital jobs can face a deepening Catch-22. As the job gets harder, relief becomes all the more pressing, but increasingly, it is a luxury. People stretch ever harder for basic escapes, which can remain tantalizingly out of reach. "I don't take personal trips," [Charlotte, North Carolina]

---

[1]Those facilitating migration, often exploiting migrants in the process.

airport tarmac worker Ms. Barber said, "explaining that it had been several years since she had taken a family vacation, and that when she did, she drove" (Smialek, 2024).

Two Developed Worlds

Economic statistics reveal two developed worlds. One experiences most of the damage while causing a tiny fraction of it. The other causes the majority of the damage while experiencing little of it. "63% of the global inequality in individual emissions is now due to a gap between low and high emitters *within* countries rather than *between* countries," (Chancel, 2022) (italics ours). Focusing on the United States, the magazine *Consumer Reports* estimates that if we remain on our current trajectory, the bill coming due for climate change could cost every American born today between $500,000 and $1 million (Medintz, 2024). That is a projected average, but realistically, this bill will be spread unevenly; those the least able to do so will bear the brunt of the cost.

This disproportionate impact takes its toll. Unlike many lawmakers, US Representative Marie Gluesenkamp Pérez (D-WA3) owns a small business with her husband. She approaches climate change in terms of how it affects her bread and butter. "My husband and I own an auto repair shop, work in the garage. When it's 117 degrees outside, I can't work, I can't pay my mortgage" (Pod Save America, 2023, 58:38–59:20).

It is not just her business. Gluesenkamp Pérez speaks of the plight of rural Americans closer to ground zero for climate change, explaining "I get my internet from a radio tower, I get my water from a well, I heat my house with wood.... It changes how you think about issues and it changes what your priorities are" (Pod Save America, 2023, 58:38–59:20). Our crackling planet looks different from this vantage point than when viewed from a distance. "When you've got a wildfire next door, it's really relevant to our timber policies" (Pod Save America, 2023, 58: 38–59:20).

The heat strikes our most vulnerable populations, including senior citizens, with particular force. Using models of sea-level rise and US Census migration data, a 2024 PNAS paper projects that many elderly folks without resources will get left behind as people migrate from coastal areas. The study's authors estimate that by 2,100, around 1.5 million people will move away from US coastal areas under a future scenario with around 2°C of warming. Add the compounding effects of projected demographic changes, and that estimate increases tenfold (Hauer et al., 2024). Despite mounting pressures to escape, not everyone can flee the heat, or pick up stakes when disaster strikes. Forecasters expect the median age of those left behind to increase by as much as 10 years over the next three quarters of a century in the geographies studied (Hauer et al., 2024). Increasingly, we live in two developed worlds.

Remember How Intense That Was?

During and after a disaster or pandemic, those with resources recover relatively well. Think of folks who can relocate readily after a flood, or those who discovered the benefits of working from home during COVID. When people with resources bounce back while others do not, it is called a K-shaped recovery. The top leg of the K, sloping up, reflects the experience of those with access to resources, alternatives, and options. The disaster becomes a bad memory, and the relocation a story. Can you get away to the country in the worst of the heat, or during a pandemic? Did you invest in backup power for when the next storm comes? If so, you are in the top leg of the K.

It's easy to forget that for those experiencing the bottom leg, recovery may not come at all. A 2020 study in the International Journal of Disaster Risk Reduction illustrates these factors and their interplay. The study focuses on vulnerability ("people are more likely to be exposed to earthquakes in seismically active areas"), susceptibility ("aging houses, roads, and machines are more prone to accidents"), and coping capacity ("poor people may lack resources to respond appropriately to a hazard") (Hansson et al., 2020).

Vulnerabilities can reinforce each other, making the bottom leg of the K particularly treacherous. Often, climate change exacerbates more than one of these vulnerabilities. Climate writer Amy Harder argues that lower-income people face a double whammy. They spend more of their paychecks on energy (heating, electricity, transportation), and they have less wherewithal to move away from disasters and extreme heat. Meanwhile, they may have far less flexibility to leave a job like our tarmac worker's or auto repair shop owner's, or they may depend for their survival on agricultural work that gets harder and harder in the heat (Harder, 2021).

Subsidies for oil, coal, and natural gas create a true Catch-22 for those in cattle class. They "have been powering our economy for decades and make up 80% of our global energy consumption (... that's barely budged in 30 years). They're plentiful and made cheap by government subsidies here and abroad." Harder explains: "They're also the main reason our planet is heating up.... Any action we take to tackle climate change is, by default, going to raise energy costs.... Those ... least able to afford it will shoulder the brunt of those costs" (Harder, 2021).

If you're used to having options, you may find it hard to imagine having so few that a disaster or infrastructure failure ruins you. You may read about folks dislocated after a storm, or worry about older or less mobile friends during an outage. At the same time, you may struggle to understand risks that don't seem to apply to you or those you care about. This can be especially true when the people most exposed live in a different part of the world. Sebastian Groh, who runs a business in Bangladesh, emphasizes this point. "Many of us are still stuck in this [mentality of] 'oh, these are the poor people, let's send them some money.'" Such funds, Groh notes, are "usually spent on consultants ... from that country [that] sends the money" (Crawford & Plavin-Masterman, 2024b).

There's a simple way to flip this model on its head. Groh continues: "The people who are closest to the problems come up with the best solutions.... And this is where the money should go, not the other way around" (Crawford & Plavin-Masterman, 2024b).

In the final part of this book, we'll focus on those solutions – and how to break open access for the most vulnerable to build alternatives to cattle class.

Chapter 3

A Number of Our Teams Made Changes to Be More Efficient and Work Better

A Good Job

To what extent will AI make our jobs better, by letting us offload the monotonous and repetitive parts to machine "intelligence?" On the other hand, to what extent will it relieve us of jobs that give our lives meaning – including those that seemed safe from previous waves of automation?

Jobs that involve rule-based responses may be especially vulnerable to replacement. Such jobs include those of the driver, medical assistant, lawyer, doctor, and coder. Generative AI could replace many white-collar jobs that, until now, evaded more conventional means of automation. It may affect advanced economies more than less developed ones, impacting 60% of jobs in advanced economies, compared to roughly 40% in emerging market economies like Brazil, India, and China, and 26% in lower-income economies (Georgieva, 2024).

Even before the revolution in generative AI, we saw a bifurcation of the kinds of jobs people do, between quality jobs for some, and jobs filled with rote tasks and limited advancement opportunities for the rest (Porter, 2019). For most of us, a quality job constitutes not a luxury, but an essential part of life. "A good job is more important than having a family, more compelling than democracy and freedom, religion, peace and so on. Those are all very important but they are now subordinate to the almighty good job" (Shawbel, 2011). When Gallup's longtime CEO, Jim Clifton, made this claim in a 2011 interview, he based it on extensive surveys the polling agency had conducted around the world.

In his book *Drive,* published in the same year, Daniel Pink distinguished between *algorithmic* tasks that follow established steps and *heuristic* tasks that require figuring out the steps (Pink, 2011, p. 27). For centuries, automation has replaced jobs that followed specific (repetitive) steps. As recently as 2011, this seemed likely to continue. Pink cited McKinsey's projections that 70% of job growth in the United States would come from heuristic work, since algorithmic work could be outsourced (Pink, 2011, p. 28).

A couple of decades on, AI platforms digest large amounts of data to figure out what needs to be done. Advanced AI agents dispense with many of our needs,

One Size Fits None, 23–27
Copyright © 2025 Alejandro Juárez Crawford and Miriam Plavin-Masterman
Published under exclusive licence by Emerald Publishing Limited
doi:10.1108/978-1-83608-660-420251004

working in tandem with workers who follow scripted rules. Does that make Pink's distinction obsolete? Most of us can remember highly visible jobs once done by people like the bank teller or toll booth operator. We may have read about jobs that disappeared behind the scenes, from the newsroom to the factory floor. When we order from Amazon or Alibaba, tens of thousands of people accomplish what hundreds of thousands used to. Gartner projects that by 2025, for more than 20% of all products, *the first human being to touch them will be the purchaser.* Everything that goes into making, storing, and shipping those products will be automated (Haight et al., 2023). In 2023, with the rise of generative AI, tech firms made massive new investments in automation, even while laying off workers to cut costs (Thorbecke, 2024). That year, AI investments were estimated at over $150 Billion (Statista, 2024), and AI startups raised nearly $50 billion (Metinko, 2024).

Sam Altman, CEO of OpenAI (the firm behind ChatGPT), has summarized the current reigning paradigm succinctly: "For me, AGI [artificial general intelligence] is the equivalent of a median human that you could hire as a co-worker" (Weil, 2023). Altman has further argued that AI can "do anything that you'd be happy with a remote coworker doing just behind a computer, which includes learning how to go be a doctor, learning how to go be a very competent coder" (Hoffman, 2023). These words highlight how much we have *already* delegated to unseen contributors behind the scenes, whether it is call center employees in another country or domestic laborers closer to home. Why should we not let algorithms learn to do this work?

As anyone delegating work knows, replacing the "slog" in our jobs – the boring, repetitive parts – can vastly expand what we accomplish. Rates of AI adoption seem to bear this out. As early as 2023, a survey found that over one-fifth of respondents regularly used AI in their work. Nearly four-fifths had some exposure, inside or outside of work (McKinsey, 2023). The International Monetary Fund (IMF) projects that AI will affect approximately four in 10 jobs worldwide, enhancing some while replacing others (Georgieva, 2024).

Though it may not be top of mind when you've just saved time using generative AI, how AI affects our jobs in the years to come hinges on which paradigm AI development follows. Whether we realize it or not, today's investments lay crucial groundwork for *how* we'll use AI. And that involves choices, though companies often frame them as competitive necessities.

Chasing Efficiency

In 2024, a year of record profits (Macrotrends, 2024), Google sent an email to employees:

> Due to changes in business needs, Google has decided to restructure operations at certain … facilities, including at the facility (if any) at which you work.… Based on this decision, we have had to make some difficult decisions about ongoing

employment of some Google employees and we regret to inform you that your position is being eliminated. (Kay, 2024)

Google framed the move as *necessary:* "We recognize how much this impacts you and regret the need to move in this direction" (Kay, 2024). What "need?" A spokesperson clarified in response to a journalist's query: "We're responsibly investing in our company's biggest priorities and the significant opportunities ahead. To best position us for these opportunities, throughout the second half of 2023, a number of our teams made changes to become more efficient and work better, and to align their resources to their biggest product priorities" (Kay, 2024).

Language about "efficiency" and "aligning resources with product priorities" can obscure the discretion investors and managers have. If you accept that faster or cheaper is a self-evident priority, it hides your option to choose what world you build. Do acquiring firms gut legendary engineering or medical capacity in favor of sourcing to the cheapest subcontractor? Do early-stage investors insist on models that "scale" at virtually no cost per additional customer? Do profitable firms with immense resources lay off workers for the sake of "efficiency?"

At first, such choices might seem straightforward. Who doesn't want to do more with less? Upon closer scrutiny, major questions lie behind them. What kind of automation amplifies our capabilities, and what kind atrophies them? When do appealing benefits at the outset lead us down a path of "good enough" solutions that make crucial systems even less responsive to our needs?

Cylon or Iron Man?

Economist and Nobel Laureate Daron Acemoglu distinguishes between automation that expands *marginal* productivity and automation that raises *average* productivity. We expand marginal capability when we amplify the capability of each worker. We raise average productivity when we do more with fewer workers (Acemoglu, 2021). A tool that *amplifies* our powers dispenses with routine or frustrating parts of a task in a way that frees us up. It feels like an extension of the body, but we keep full discretion over how we move. By contrast, a tool that automates people *out* of the equation – like an ATM or autonomous truck – is designed to allow a few operators to do the work of many.

This distinction shows up in popular fiction, in the figures of the automaton and the exoskeleton. Famous fictional automatons include the Cylon and the Terminator. Popular exoskeletons include Iron Man and the Caterpillar Power Loader from the movie *Aliens* (Sofge, 2010). The automaton replaces the functions of a person, such as a laborer, sentry, pilot, soldier, or attendant. The exoskeleton amplifies the user's capability, adding strength or providing insights from the environment that the human user can interpret and use.

The distinction exists in other parts of life too. In 2023, TV writers went on strike, in part, to negotiate protections for their rights to *use* AI, rather than being replaced by it. A Brookings Institution report points to this as the operative distinction in the contract the artists won: "The contract explicitly spells out that

AI is not itself a writer competing with humans, but rather a tool for writers' beneficial use. To the extent that AI is used, the regulations specify that AI should complement the work of writers instead of replacing them" (Kinder, 2024).

In Ghana, energy researchers used a computer simulation linked to AI to determine the best way to move forward with renewable energy sources (Byrne, 2024). They found that if Ghana expanded solar and wind without considering local context, they would end up with unpredictable floods caused by supplemental hydropower turning on and off to balance the needs of the energy grid. They needed to carefully plan solar and wind projects to take this into account. They employed AI in an attempt to ensure that the renewable energy produced in various parts of Ghana could be deployed where and when needed.

The researchers were endeavoring to use AI on the exoskeleton model, to amplify their power and extend their reach. As with any automation, this carried risks. For example, the AI might have baked in existing assumptions, leading the researchers to miss alternatives. It also brought significant benefits. The researchers and energy planners extended their marginal productivity as they worked to minimize damage to rivers and those living nearby, while increasing the use of renewable energy countrywide.

Algorithms do a great job of sifting through reams of data in ways that prove incredibly time-consuming for human beings. Organizations ranging from Amazon to Domino's Pizza and from Air France/KLM to Georgia Tech (Bhanu, 2023) have implemented chatbots to check on orders, pick seats, or choose appropriate classes. When we use AI as an "exoskeleton" to amplify our efforts, it can quickly execute activities we might otherwise struggle to perform. Many of us depend on automated recommendations to find routes, restaurants, films, jobs, and even romantic partners. The authors used generative AI to come up with preliminary lists of books on related topics when submitting the proposal for this book.

Convenience turns into frustration when the algorithm *fails to understand the context*. For example, when the authors launched their podcast, *What if Instead?* the publisher used an AI algorithm to voice the intro and outro for each episode. Lacking context, the algorithm insisted for at least a year on pronouncing the name Plavin with a soft "a" (as if it rhymed with the "o" in "model"). Here, context is everything; the author's Latvian ancestors might well have pronounced it the way the AI did, but her family pronounces it differently now in the United States. With more data, would we expect the AI to gain that context? Maybe. In some situations, large language models (LLMs) generate uncannily useful results. Still, the more precise the context, the more likely that the LLM will get it wrong, and produce a *generic* result.

Our most resourceful and innovative solutions require questioning or upending assumptions. Should we count on software to do the critical thinking for us, about the mass of assumptions on which it was trained? How many people already use AI to generate content with minimal or no critical review?

Douglas Hofstadter describes receiving a message from a fan of his book *Gödel, Escher, Bach.* The fan had asked AI to explain why Hofstadter had written his classic. Receiving an explanation, he forwarded it to Hofstadter, voicing excitement about the results. In response, Hofstadter argued: "I would say that that [AI-generated] text, in sharp contrast to what I myself wrote in the book's 20th-anniversary preface, consists only in generic platitudes and fluffy hand-waving." He then articulated why this concerned him more broadly: "Large language models, although ... mind-bogglingly impressive in many ways, do not think up original ideas;... they glibly and slickly rehash words and phrases 'ingested' by them in their training phase, which draws on untold millions of web sites, books, articles, etc." (Hofstadter, 2023).

The crucial question is one of *responsiveness*, being able to respond meaningfully to specific situations. AI can synthesize, digest, and spit out results, faster and often better than we could. But as soon as we stop thinking critically about what AI gives us, poorly stitched "seams" often show. As Hofstadter writes: "At first glance, the products of today's LLMs may appear convincing and true, but one often finds, on careful analysis, that they fall apart at the seams" (Hofstadter, 2023).

Chapter 4

The Blank Page Problem

The Rote Stuff

What does automating job search have to do with writing a book using ChatGPT?

Today, LinkedIn uses Artificial Intelligence (AI) agents to handle various tasks, from turning "scrappy notes and thoughts . . . into longer job descriptions [,] to sourcing candidates and engaging with them" (Lunden, 2024). Amid the convenience, tech founder Joe Procopio sees trouble brewing:

> A company starts using AI to screen candidates, which results in poorly matched candidates, which results in candidates having to apply to more jobs to get seen, which results in candidates using AI themselves to get past the AI screening, which results in an avalanche of completely mismatched candidates for every single posted job, none of which get filled. (Procopio, 2024)

LinkedIn founder Reid Hoffman used AI to draft what he called "the first book written with GPT-4" (Hoffman, 2023). He discusses this on a podcast with Sam Altman, whose company built the AI engine Hoffman used. Both argue passionately that AI will amplify our potential. They believe it will serve as an exoskeleton: freeing up our creativity, enabling us to find "flow," and bringing us joy. It will do so, they argue, by taking on the elusive parts, like that blank page, and by knocking out the monotonous ones. Hoffman stresses: "By moving it out of . . . the rote stuff, you can also not just make it in the more creative stuff – and it's always what some people [are] fearful of – but also the more joyful parts of work, and I think that transformation of joy is again amplifying human beings" (Hoffman, 2023).

"I deeply believe this," Altman agrees. "It's a little too early to declare victory on it, but it certainly seems like people stay in the flow state much more, stay in the parts of the job they enjoy much more." His optimism is resounding – it's only "a little" too early to declare victory. "AI is, like, good at doing the repetitive stuff that most of us find a little bit monotonous" (Hoffman, 2023). What could be more appealing?

One Size Fits None, 29–35
Copyright © 2025 Alejandro Juárez Crawford and Miriam Plavin-Masterman
Published under exclusive licence by Emerald Publishing Limited
doi:10.1108/978-1-83608-660-420251005

Technology's promise has long been to do the boring parts for us. Why start with a blank page, when AI can solve the "problem" for us, as Hoffman says? For that matter, why finish this sentence, when an algorithm will make it "good enough?" How many of us have used AI to finish a sentence in an email or a text message? It didn't say exactly what we meant, perhaps. But who has time to go back and change it, if it more or less conveys the gist?

Use It or Lose It

For many of us, the point of a text message is speed. Precise word choice goes out the window, right after punctuation. When the bar for precision is low, why not let the autocomplete or autoresponse do its thing? For a book, the bar might be higher, but then, AI's authoring capabilities keep getting better. So maybe we delegate some parts of writing the book, but reserve others?

This is where Hoffman's idea of the blank page problem and letting AI take care of "the rote stuff" gets interesting. Where exactly do we draw the line? How habit-forming, in a pinch, does such delegating become? If that seems like an idle question, talk to someone who has submitted work recently, facing a tight deadline and tough standards for grammar and usage. AI can already do speed better than any of us, and grammar and usage better than most. Where formalities matter, that large language model, with its capacity to source from so much text, already seems able to pull the phrases that fit the context. It's hard enough to find the words for what we mean, much less make them fit formal requirements. As the interface gets better at approximating what we must have meant, what will remain important enough that we'll take the trouble to worry about word choice?

How much of what you mean to say will you cede to the AI? To what extent are you – your coworkers, your students, your kids – already getting used to relying on it? What do we lose when we delegate obstacles and hurdles like the blank page? In physical exercise, cables and machines remove the challenge of balancing. But what happens to us when we let the equipment exercise for us?

It's, You Know, Your Companion

When tech does a "good enough" job at activities that have depended on human beings, the profit potential is phenomenal, as Elon Musk emphasized at Tesla's 2024 shareholder meeting. Musk spoke of the Optimus robots he was then planning to begin selling, and not just for factory work. He gushed: "It's, you know, your companion, it can be at your house, it can sort of babysit your kids, it could teach them.... It, you know, it can do factory stuff" (Novak, 2024). In his comments, Musk applied a software business model to the fundamental activities human beings conduct. He explicitly presented this in terms of its potential to drive extraordinary growth, claiming it would lead the company to a $25 trillion market capitalization.[1] If he were proved right, Tesla would soon be worth more than half the *combined* value, at the time he made the comments, of the firms in the S&P 500.[2]

Musk gushed: "You'll just literally be able to talk to it and say 'please do this task' or 'I'm gonna show you something. Now do that thing that I'm showing you'" (Novak, 2024). Musk went on to claim that humanoid robots will outnumber human beings and take on tasks throughout our lives, presenting this as a clear win. "It will be able to play the piano. So it's really like, wow" (Novak, 2024).

Automated player pianos are hardly new; mechanical pianos have existed since the 19th century and had a market since the early 20th. What those mechanical pianos could never do is pause slightly longer, before the next phrase, to respond dynamically to the listener's smallest reactions, the way live performers do. Player pianos can't be *responsive*. Today, AI might achieve a "barely good enough" responsiveness that leaves us cold, without our knowing why.

A number of movies released by streaming services have been described as algorithm-driven, and not in a good way (Aaron, 2024). It's as if the studio took an idea for a twist, combined it with a recent movie trend, added a reputable cast, and spit something out. What appears is the veneer of a movie – until you scratch the surface and the plot falls apart, since the algorithm couldn't distinguish between story and plot. To paraphrase EM Forster (1956), "'The king died and then the queen died' is a story. 'The king died, and then the queen died of grief' is a plot." The story is what happens and the plot is why.

Will this change as AI gets up the learning curve? Or will we lose the plot further, the more we delegate to large language models? Apple faced public backlash after a 2024 iPad ad called "Crush," in which a trash compactor crushes musical instruments, video game controllers, a turntable, and a sculpture, to reveal a new iPad. The company's promise has long been to extend the capability of people to make their dreams possible – to "think different(ly)." Historically, fans have often greeted new Apple products with passion (Rettner, 2010). This time, Apple appeared to strike a false note. Many consumers and artists were appalled at images of Apple crushing the instruments of human expression (Beres & Warzel, 2024). The popular outcry led the company to take down the ad and promise to stop running it.

While Apple's ad was just a video, it spoke to real-world concerns. The TV writers' strike described in the last chapter had occurred only a year before. Would these writers have fought so hard for contractual protections against replacement by AI, had they not faced the risk of machines doing the writing at little or no cost per additional episode? If we can invest once, then produce endless content for nothing and get people used to consuming it, what a flywheel! It could spin continuously.

---

[1]What the company as a whole will be worth on the market if you add up the value of all its shares.
[2]The S&P is a weighted index of 500 leading publicly traded companies.

The Quiet Part Out Loud

Former OpenAI CTO Mira Murati faced pushback in June 2024, after conceding that "some creative jobs maybe will go away, but maybe they shouldn't have been there in the first place" at a talk at Dartmouth College's engineering school (Dartmouth Engineering, 2024).

Murati said the quiet part out loud, treating creativity like an interchangeable input. This takes the automaton model to its logical extension. It raises the question of whether Altman's rhapsodizing about offloading the *boring* parts might actually be about the *expensive* parts. The expensive parts often comprise quality jobs – the ones that give purpose to our lives, if Gallup is to be believed.

Murati's suggestion that jobs that disappear will do so because they "shouldn't have been there in the first place" reveals a blind spot. How much human creativity starts as something no one wants, only to become indispensable to a small audience or a large one? As a society, we are good at making junk – fast fashion, fast food, trash television, single-use items, etc. All those cheap, low-quality things provide income for people, who in turn pay rent or a mortgage and buy more things. At first blush, we might excuse the mentality Murati revealed as that of a stereotypical artist's parent, failing to see why their kid hasn't picked a major that translates into obvious job prospects. But when it's the then-CTO of OpenAI speaking, the implications are more telling.

What is gained by removing the struggle of the blank page, and what is lost? Writers, musicians, and artists we now revere often *failed* to observe the conventions of their day (Berger, 1972, pp. 53–56). They *departed* from then-dominant practices, but AI trains on our leading practices. Its creations and "hallucinations" might depart from those practices in unexpected directions; how will we distinguish between results that fail to please and brilliant departures? Generative AI can *produce* art that people value. It's unclear whether it can *depart* from what we have learned to value.

Struggling to Be People Without Assistance

We're tempted by assistance saying what we mean to say and creating what we wish to create. We're also regularly offered a little help deciding what we want. When we gave up physical QWERTY keyboards like those on Blackberry devices, we gained larger screens for browsing and watching media. We also entered an era in which we ceded active control, opening up opportunities for third parties to use our attention for their purposes.

Most digital tools now offer recommendations and default views. These often feature what the provider wishes to promote, including both products and opportunities to capture our data. For example, newer interfaces for the Amazon Kindle or today's Google may lead users to the product Amazon thinks you should try, or contain a hyperlink designed to give Google your data as you click on the link. To avoid this, you need to invest a ton of energy in changing defaults. While defaults might appear to be neutral options you can choose to decline, research into "choice architecture" has shown that users consistently favor the default (Camilleri & Larrick, 2015).

Take away your discretion, and you're a passenger. Being a passenger can be pleasant – sit back and enjoy the flight. It can also atrophy the capacity to pilot. As early as 2013, the writer Nassim Nicholas Taleb refers to the "recently observed effect in aeronautics that the automation of airplanes is under-challenging pilots, making flying too comfortable for them, dangerously comfortable" (Taleb, 2013, pp. 62–63). This goes beyond just automated triggers and warnings, to the disengagement of our attention:

> Dulling of the pilot's attention and skills from too little challenge is ... causing deaths from flying accidents. Part of the problem is a Federal Aviation Administration (FAA) regulation that forced the industry to increase its reliance on automated flying. But ... the same FAA ... has recently found that pilots often "abdicate too much responsibility to automated systems." (Taleb, 2013, pp. 62–63)

Are we destined, like Lieutenant Madison in the movie *Galaxy Quest*, for roles where we repeat whatever the computer says (Parisot, 1999)? Many of us have allowed once-critical skills to atrophy – remembering numbers, learning routes, or performing calculations. Many who grew up before cell phones used to remember the phone numbers of good friends or loved ones, and now don't. Does being relieved of the need to remember sequences of digits atrophy brain power, or free it up?

It used to be that if you asked directions to a place in someone's neighborhood, the friend might tell you all the turns to get there. How many of us can do that today, in the age of GPS? Remembering street numbers and turns may seem trivial, chores that free up brain power when we don't have to do them anymore. At which point do we delegate too much? Entrepreneur and philanthropist Péter Küllői asks audiences whether they would accept a chip in their brain. Most say no. He then asks how many spent more than 6 hours with their phones out of easy reach. Very few hands go up (Küllői, 2019).

Tyler Austin Harper quotes Whitney Wolfe Herd, founder and executive chair of the dating app Bumble. Herd claims that "If you want to get really out there, there is a world where your dating concierge could go and date for you with other dating concierges.... And then you don't have to talk to 600 people. It will then scan all of San Francisco for you and say, these are the three people you really ought to meet" (Harper, 2024).

Harper takes this to its logical conclusion. "Hypothetical AI dating concierges sound silly, and they are not exactly humanity's greatest threat. But we might ... think of the Bumble founder's bubbly sales pitch as a canary in the coal mine, a harbinger of a world of algorithms that leave people struggling to be people without assistance" (Harper, 2024).

Beyond the loss of skills and intellectual capabilities, to what extent do we risk losing our capacity to distinguish between what we want and what a platform leads us to choose? If you've ever faced a sales pitch designed to exploit your weaknesses, you'll recognize the difference between what you want when you are being manipulated and what you intend. This difference is at play in every version of junk food your brain consumes. Social media companies use sophisticated algorithms to trigger dopamine release (Haynes, 2018). They play upon our cognitive biases to engage us with content that triggers these biases (Menczer, 2021). Slightly more than 62% of the world's population uses social media, "on average for over 2 hours a day at least as of April 2024" (Chaffey, 2024). So many people watch videos designed to make them angry or upset, or obsessively check daily news developments. This, argues Taleb, represents little more than "noise" keeping us on the edge of our seats to see what happened, while more important developments escape our notice (Taleb, 2013, p. 174).

Mediocrity at Scale

As AI trains on what we do, it may learn to mimic and expand upon the weaknesses of the shoddy work product, the problem employee, the biased hiring manager, or the internet troll. Already, AI agents and platforms will not let you order Mountain Dew at the drive-through (Sanders, 2024); accidentally give you food poisoning by telling you to drink cleaning supplies (Sarlin, 2024); and recommend adding nontoxic glue to your pizza to ensure the cheese won't slide off (Notopoulos, 2024). AI replicates the friend who encourages you in the blandest terms ("Don't worry Kev, these things happen"), won't give you constructive criticism, and perpetuates your worst instincts (Roose, 2024). Students turn in all-but-plagiarized assignments, while various users spread dis- and misinformation.

As AI gets more powerful, these phenomena could easily get worse. In the quest to replace the "median human," we risk replicating mediocrity at scale, unresponsiveness with a smile. It's all too easy to go down a road where we train machines to repeat and recombine our most insipid thoughts. Here, we use "insipid" to describe the limitations of early generative AI, from frequent "hallucinations" to the tone-deaf answers offered by Kevin Roose's artificial companion on the *Hard Fork* episode "Meet Kevin's AI Friends" (Roose et al., 2024). More than that, we use the word to describe teaching AI to perpetuate the most predictable things we do.

Are You Being Served?

Many old stories center around a bad bargain. A helper magically relieves someone of a thorny problem (The Pied Piper, Rumpelstiltskin), or magic gives us seemingly unlimited access to what we used to struggle for (King Midas). Science fiction often updates this idea, where tech replaces magic.

The Altmans of the world promise an AI future in which we get powerful exoskeletons without ceding too much of the process. Will this end up being a bad bargain, as in these stories? To make it otherwise would require intensive investment in making systems responsive on our terms. At present, our tech sector, finance industry, elected representatives, and other key groups are failing to make that investment. Automation's recent history should not make us optimistic. As Acemoglu has argued, "a handful of companies with business models focused on automation came to dominate the economy. And government tax policy started favoring capital and automation. Whatever the exact mechanisms, technology became less favorable to labor and more focused on automation" (Acemoglu, 2021). Leading models for AI may be about to accelerate this tendency in ways we've never seen before. But what led capital to favor such models in the first place?

Chapter 5

There's No Such Thing as a Free Flywheel or Hockey Stick

But Can It Scale?

How have unresponsive models taken over so many industries? In this chapter, we pull back the curtain.

Previous chapters described the spread of business models that prioritize serving as many people as possible – while engaging the efforts of as few as possible. We saw how this keeps the systems we use from responding to our needs, until it becomes commonplace to go from crisis to crisis while reaching for forms of escape.

By design, unresponsive models satisfy generic needs cheaply and abundantly. They minimize and strictly program human interaction, with its capacity to respond to variations, or remove it altogether. These models squeeze human variation out of industry after industry, reserving it for premium payers. Silicon Valley demonstrated that it was possible to satisfy many people's needs without doing additional work again to satisfy the next user. This proved so profitable that *investors increasingly look for businesses that work the way software does.*

Many have come to expect the software-like returns this kind of model promises. "It's great, *but can it scale?*" is a standard challenge in a venture capital pitch meeting. For many investors, the expectation of software-like scalability is baked into the promises they make to those who provide the funds they invest. This governs which kinds of solutions get the capital they need. Across industries, innovators have learned to promise and seek "hockey stick" growth. The hockey stick refers to the rising line on a graph of money coming in, where it shoots up sharply like the handle of a hockey stick, after a short period of burning through cash to set up the ascent. When an entrepreneur claims, as in the example we quoted in the last chapter, that robots that can babysit your kids will drive his company to a $25 trillion valuation, he's promising hockey stick growth.

One Size Fits None, 37–43

Copyright © 2025 Alejandro Juárez Crawford and Miriam Plavin-Masterman
Published under exclusive licence by Emerald Publishing Limited
doi:10.1108/978-1-83608-660-420251006

More Revenue, Same Cost

A company like Spotify or Slack gets new revenue for each subscription. But the company doesn't need to *do* anything additional for each new one, besides have enough cloud servers available and (sometimes) arrange tech support for users that get past the automated chat. The company must make improvements to its core product, of course; it updates software with new functionality or makes deals with content providers. Still, the company spends money *once* on these activities for all customers using a given software product. When a company can serve millions (or billions) of individuals this way (or support thousands of businesses doing so in turn), profits can go through the roof. That's because the company doesn't have to build features again for each customer.

Economists call the amount of money spent to serve the next customer "marginal" cost. A model that scales in this way pushes the marginal cost per customer served as close to zero as possible. Meta, the parent company of Facebook and Instagram, embodies this dream. As of December 2024, the company reported serving more than 45,000 "active daily people" per employee (Meta Investor Relations, 2025). Imagine paying one employee for every 45,000 users, while the software (and those users) do the rest of the work. That's the dream of scalability, at close to zero marginal cost.

Models that do something once, then sell it to millions, didn't start with software. Once Coca-Cola develops the formula for a new flavor, the cost of sugar water and a plastic bottle for each customer served is relatively minimal. McDonald's releases a new menu item once, and then its franchises everywhere serve up the item in a relatively automated fashion (Buehler, 2023; Ganti, 2024). With software, the deal got even sweeter. Coke still needs to deal with all those vending machines and supermarket channels, McDonald's, all those stores. With software, *it's pretty much just the formula*. Once people and organizations are on a certain platform, it can be a huge pain for them to switch.

As software expanded across industries, this became the dream of many investors. Early on, when Microsoft or Adobe released a new version of Windows or Acrobat, you had to buy a box of discs with a unique license. The company had to print up discs and get them into stores, but at a sliver of the price you paid each time you upgraded or added new software. The core principle was the same: Microsoft could sell the new version of Windows to millions of customers while making that version of the software *once*.

The *blade* of the hockey stick, the part along the ground, represents the cost of developing a new product. As users multiply and the product takes off, revenues grow dramatically, rising up and to the right, the way a hockey stick's shaft angles up from the ice. If you're an investor, what's not to love? You invest early, to get the software company past the flat part, before it makes its steep ascent. Successive rounds of investment make new hockey sticks possible as the company releases the next big product or feature.

Where the hockey stick promises growth once the initial work is done, the "flywheel effect" captures the idea of putting something in motion that keeps going on its own. Once it starts, a flywheel keeps on spinning, with little to no further effort required. Management guru Jim Collins and others popularized the application of this idea to business; it may have taken root after Amazon founder Jeff Bezos wrote it on a napkin (Cushing, 2021). Like the hockey stick returns that often go with them, flywheels can be beautiful things. Indeed, businesses may struggle if the value they deliver has to be created from scratch each time. But what happens when we start looking for flywheels everywhere?

Flywheel or Bust

Today, if a business *doesn't* work like software, it can struggle to raise capital. Once flywheels and hockey sticks become requirements, it gets tempting to force them onto industries and businesses that lack them. Some of the more infamous entrepreneurial scandals of our day illustrate this well. Why would experienced investors buy into the idea that We Work's office real estate business could scale like software? Why would smart people accept, without rigorous and diligent inspection, that Theranos could diagnose hundreds of diseases from a single drop of blood? The press often focused on these firms' founders, but what led our system for fueling innovation to put capital and reputations behind them? Why did so many investors buy what these entrepreneurs were selling?

While not every business fakes its diagnostics or inflates its growth potential, these examples illustrate the pressure now placed on industries that don't work much like software at all. When investors look for flywheels everywhere, that pressure affects not just startups, but hospitals and schools, manufacturers, and governments. It's one thing to use a platform like Facebook when there's one employee per tens of thousands of people, quite another when your health or your education depends on this type of model.

Starting in the 2010s, argues fintech executive Henry Joyce, venture capitalists sought returns through "blitzscaling." They would invest in a business that promised flywheel effects using minimal assets, then scale up fast: think Uber drivers and passengers or Airbnb hosts and guests. Though the business carried few assets, users got value from *other* users. In many ways, this applied to other industries the logic that enables each Meta employee to "serve" 45,000 users. When users serve each other, the company doesn't need to invest in cars, hotels, or content.

As this proceeded, investors began to expect scenarios in which revenue grew wildly based on small investments. You might not have gotten in early on Facebook or Airbnb, but you could look for investments that similarly multiplied the people they could serve *using fewer assets or people*. This focus on serving more people with less came to affect industries far removed from software and "sharing economy" models like Airbnb. Consider what's happened to US healthcare as investors have focused on serving as many people as possible as "efficiently" as possible.

Hungry Hungry Hippos

Across the US healthcare system, private equity (PE) firms have bought up hospitals and doctors' practices (Morris et al., 2024; Weber, 2022). Over 400 US hospitals are now owned by PE firms (Nocera & McLean, 2023). PE-owned hospitals include approximately 8% of private hospitals and slightly more than 20% of proprietary for-profit hospitals. Over 25% of PE-owned hospitals serve rural populations (Private Equity Stakeholder Project, 2024).

PE investors have scaled back staffing, hours, and services, then loaded up hospitals with debt, weighing them down with rent payments on buildings they used to own. By forcing them to do more with less in the name of efficiency, this model often squeezes the responsiveness out of a hospital system. This practice does not end with making large hospitals do more with less. PE firms have invested in physician practices, too, across multiple specialties at an accelerating pace. These investments increased from 75 deals in 2012 to over 500 deals in 2021.

By "rolling up" competing players in an industry, PE firms go beyond driving down costs. When a single firm controls a large share of local medical providers, it can also raise prices, since it's effectively the only game in town. A 2023 study of 10 physician practice specialties (Scheffler et al., 2023) found price increases associated with PE firms' acquisition, ranging from 16% in oncology practices to 4% in primary care and dermatology practices. A second survey from 2022 analyzed PE acquisitions in ophthalmology, gastroenterology, and dermatology and found that "practices charged insurance an extra 20%, or an average of $71, more after a private equity acquisition" (Singh et al., 2022).

Rather than constituting the exception, this kind of market power has become the norm in many areas. In nearly 30% of United States metropolitan statistical areas (MSAs), a single PE firm controls more than 30% of market share. In nearly 15% of MSAs, a single PE firm has a market share of over 50% (Scheffler et al., 2023).

PE acquisitions can diminish patient experience even as system costs rise. This is what we mean by squeezing the responsiveness out of an industry. PE voracity can spread unresponsive models quickly across a given industry, especially where tech makes it possible to go beyond garden-variety "efficiencies" to implement software-powered flywheels for an industry. After this process does its work, it seeks the next target. The PE practice of "flipping," or reselling within five years, continues in the background while firms look for the next category out of which they can squeeze value (Patil et al., 2023).

Consumers may wonder why their eye exam experience (for example) seems to change everywhere except for at a few local holdouts. Sometimes the shift gets attention – as when local drug stores disappeared throughout the economy. Other times it happens in the background until we get used to it. How much does the average person think, between visits to the optometrist, about how the experience has changed? Anyway, you need glasses, so "whatcha gonna do?"

Chat With Our Virtual Assistant

Over the past five years, telehealth went from limited adoption in the United States, through widespread use during COVID lockdowns out of necessity, to being pushed on patients broadly for its efficiency. Since 2023, nearly three-quarters of US physicians offer telehealth (Henry, 2023). Many practices are going further, incorporating chatbots into service delivery. AI powered a quarter of such chats, while 26% used more limited rule-based chatbots, and 42% used both models (Morris, 2023).

The most common uses for medical chatbots include administrative tasks like patient appointment scheduling. When a medical system allows chatbots to function outside business hours (which most do), patients can request refills, referrals, or medical histories without the doctor's office having to pay a person to handle these tasks. However, a 2024 survey found that "some doctors are turning to [free] tools intended for non-clinical uses [ChatGPT, etc.] to make clinical decisions. With no standardized guidelines, lagging physician training, and regulators racing to try to keep up with rapidly changing technology, guardrails to protect patients appear to be years behind current rates of utilization" (Gliadkovskaya, 2024).

When it comes to health, even an unlikely mistake can be incredibly costly. Using chatbots to carry out administrative tasks makes sense, but over three-quarters "of physicians surveyed [in the 2024 survey] reported using general-purpose large language models in clinical decision-making. More than 60% of physicians reported using LLMs like ChatGPT to check drug interactions, while more than half use them for diagnosis support. Almost half use them to generate clinical documentation, and more than 40% use them for treatment planning. Seventy percent use them for patient education and literature search" (Gliadkovskaya, 2024). In a separate Forrester Research survey, 63% of providers said they expect AI to have a large impact in predicting patient outcomes (Forrester Research, 2024).

These statistics may be more disturbing because ChatGPT barely passed the US Medical Licensing Exam (Varanasi, 2023). ChatGPT, like other general-purpose LLMs, is trained on publicly available information online. This means paywalled medical and scientific journals are left out of LLM training, but Reddit and other scientifically unverified sites on the internet are in the training data.

Today's algorithms will almost certainly improve at providing plausible responses. That does not mean those responses will more effectively meet needs in particular situations. We could easily be entering a world in which we delegate increasingly to AI, and its responses become ever more convincing while failing spectacularly to meet many of our needs (Zitron, 2024b, 2024h).

Many doctors are not all that worried; in the 2023 survey we mentioned earlier, over three-quarters of them said they were confident in their chatbot's ability to accurately assess patient symptoms right now. Nearly half considered ChatGPT a useful tool for doctors, no adjustments needed. And 77% believe AI-powered chatbots will develop to the point of being able to safely treat patients within the next 10 years (Morris, 2023). We are likely to find out.

None of Us Realized This Had Happened

As PE firms buy up hospital chains and physician practices, squeeze them for profits, and saddle them with debt, they leave behind less responsive systems. Along the way, a hospital system can lose its focus on serving patients or communities. A system works well when returns on an investment come from delivering superior results to the people the system serves. In this case, the purpose of the system may change – to delivering results for investors at the expense of serving patients. Patients pay more and get less. The distance between the service providers and those they serve grows, and the PE firm collects its profits and moves on.

There is no such thing as a free flywheel or hockey stick. When we try to wring hockey stick returns from hospital systems, patient care gets automated and reduced, giving public health a massive hit or handing customers and future taxpayers giant bills. As the use of AI expands, this risk could multiply. Consider a situation managed *without* AI. One of the authors was with his father in the hospital for a condition that can be life-threatening but is treatable if addressed within a matter of hours. The doctors responded with urgency but agreed that moving forward required a certain test. Then the wheels stopped moving. It turned out – the doctors were as frustrated as anyone – that this happened because the patient had been "lost" in the hospital's intersecting systems. As the doctor explained after "finding" him again and moving things forward, "I'm so glad you were here with him. None of us realized this had happened."

A well-designed AI might have been able to alert hospital staff to the breakdown. Indeed, AI has powerful healthcare applications. For example, it helps wearable devices monitor and manage vital levels for at-risk patients, and can alert caregivers to the need for interventions. By the same token, imagine trying to explain to an AI nurse that your father has been lost in the system. Imagine trying to tell an AI agent that a diagnosis is wrong, or that you know from experience that a suggested medication will make your condition worse. Or try to get an insurance company, which already uses AI to approve claims, to pay for a procedure you need.

In a podcast episode focused on the 2024 killing of health insurer UnitedHealthcare (UHC)'s CEO Brian Thompson, co-hosts Trevor Noah and Christiana Mbakwe Medina discuss lawsuits surrounding UHC's practices for denying healthcare claims. Noah explains: "they had … AI software a while ago … that was basically approving or denying claims … and then they found that it was making [a lot of] mistake[s], and they kept it because they [knew people rarely appeal denied claims,] and were making record profits" (Noah et al., 2024). In noting the public reaction to the UHC CEO's killing, the hosts question what it means when "the system doesn't care about you," asking "if all the people are against the system, who is the system for?" (Noah et al., 2024).

We opened this book with a surgeon being called out of the OR, during a preapproved procedure, to further justify it to UHC. That happened *after* the CEO's shooting. If your incentives no longer reward taking care of people, the system's purpose has changed (Benjamin & Komlos, 2021). When it means wringing the responsiveness from a system, the hunt for hockey stick returns can create a dystopian experience. The healthcare industry is just one example. Consider food. In the 1980s, United States regulators aimed "to reward the biggest retail chains for their efficiency. Instead, [their policies] devastated poor and rural communities by pushing out grocery stores and inflating the cost of food.... Once independent stores closed, chains ... could count on people to schlep across town to other locations" (Mitchell, 2024).

Consumers bear the cost of this unresponsiveness. "Today,... many Deanwood [Washington, D.C] residents travel to a Safeway outside the neighborhood to shop. This particular Safeway has had such persistent issues with expired meat and rotting produce that some locals have taken to calling it the 'UnSafeway'. Yet, without alternatives, people keep shopping there" (Mitchell, 2024).

When you try to make everything work like software, you pack people more tightly into cattle class.

Part II

A Feature, Not a Bug

As you will no doubt be aware, the plans for development of the outlying regions of the Galaxy require the building of a hyperspatial express route through your star system. And regrettably, your planet is one of those scheduled for demolition. The process will take slightly less than two of your Earth minutes. Thank you. – *The Hitchhiker's Guide to the Galaxy* (Adams, 1979, p. 57)

Chapter 6

Those Other Countries Are Closer Than They Appear

Dry Conditions

Climate change functions as a catalyst that sets other crises in motion. Amar Rahman, global head of climate resilience at Zurich Resilience Solutions, explains: "When temperature rises in a country,... it can reduce water availability and ... quality. This may increase the spread of disease and raise the likelihood of drought leading to crop failures that will reduce incomes and food supplies. All this can potentially lead to social disruption and political instability" (McAllister, 2024).

Rahman argues that we may have already seen an example of this domino effect in Syria:

> The desertification of formerly fertile farming land between 2006 and 2010 meant crop yields plummeted, 800,000 people lost their income and 85 percent of the country's livestock died. As people lost their livelihoods, food prices soared, and 1.5 million rural workers moved to the city to find jobs. Those left behind facing poverty were an easy target for recruiters from the Islamic State. (McAllister, 2024)

While climate change alone didn't cause the Syrian civil war with its exodus of millions, it may have created the conditions for it. According to the United Nations High Commissioner for Refugees (UNHCR), by 2020, 95% of all conflict displacements occurred in countries vulnerable or highly vulnerable to climate change (McAllister, 2024).

If we stay on our current course, it's reasonable to expect seemingly separate global crises, including disasters, wars, famines, and mass migration, to expand. Humanity is already headed deep into the red zone. Existing policies and actions lead us well past the threshold we introduced in Part I, to 2.5°C above preindustrial levels, as Fig. 2 shows. Beyond that threshold, every decimal point rise triggers chain reactions and compounding effects. These include unprecedented

One Size Fits None, 47–55
Copyright © 2025 Alejandro Juárez Crawford and Miriam Plavin-Masterman
Published under exclusive licence by Emerald Publishing Limited
doi:10.1108/978-1-83608-660-420251007

wildfires, which burn carbon-reducing forests and release that carbon into the atmosphere; melting ice caps, which raise water levels everywhere, and extreme heat, which makes already-hot parts of the world uninhabitable for human beings and other creatures.

Historic Emissions and Projected Warming, 1990-2100

Based on pledges and current policies (adapted from Climate Analytics and New Climate Institute)

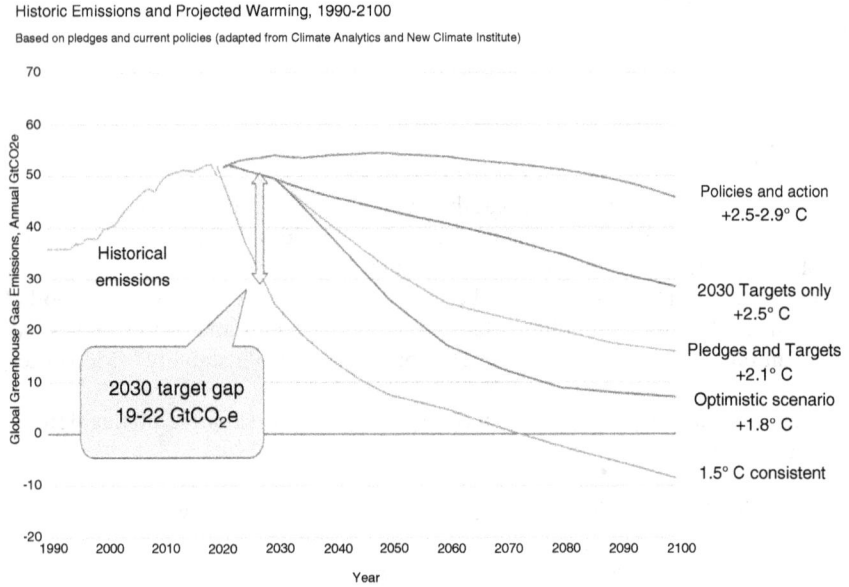

Fig. 2.   2100 Warming Projections, as of December 2023. *Source:* The authors, adapted from Climate Analytics and New Climate Institute data, 2023.

If the world reduces emissions in line with current policies and action, we're projected to reach 2.5–2.9°C above preindustrial levels by 2100. Consider the effect expected levels of warming could have on hunger, displacement, health, and economics if we stay on our current course.

Growing Hunger

The World Food Program estimates that an increase of 2°C in average global temperatures (above preindustrial levels) may put 189 million people at risk.[1]

---

[1]Preindustrial levels provide a baseline for the climate before humans started pumping trillions of tons of greenhouse gases into the atmosphere each year. In Fig. 2, we express these in carbon equivalent units, where the current annual level is just over 50 million kilotons.

That's the *optimistic* scenario, based on pledges and targets we're on track to miss (WFP, 2021).

For each percentage point increase after that, the calamity multiplies several times over. A further 2°C temperature rise could trigger a tenfold increase in hunger risk, leaving almost 2 billion people without basic sustenance.

Changing precipitation and temperature patterns linked to climate change also affect food security by reducing agricultural production (IPCC, 2022). Sudden events like hurricanes or floods as well as slower events like droughts and rising sea levels can destroy infrastructure and increase food insecurity, expanding migration waves (IOM, 2024).

Economically, the cost to incumbents might seem high, but the cost of continuing on our current trajectory will be extraordinary. A new study of 1,600 world regions says that by 2050, the climate crisis will cost the world economy $38 trillion annually (Kotz et al., 2024), and result in an income reduction of nearly 20%. Most estimates focus on the effects of rising average temperatures, increasing temperature variability, and rainfall changes. Storms and wildfires are more challenging to model but are expected to increase that total.

Public attention tends to focus on the latest storm, wildfire, or disease. Rallying to address one of these crises, as crucial as that is, can obscure the extent to which they are connected, and contribute to interacting threats. In this sense, flooding, disease, heat, and wildfires are like the heads of the hydra. Cut one off, while two more grow elsewhere, and you don't beat the monster.

We've seen this movie before. Climate changes disrupted the sixth-century Roman Empire, primarily through disease outbreaks. The infamous Plague of Justinian killed tens of millions of people around the Mediterranean, and almost half the population of the Roman Empire.

A 2024 *Science Advances* study links the ancient plague outbreak and other pandemics in the Roman Empire to climate change (Zonneveld et al., 2024). The study's authors suggest that pandemics may have resulted from disruptions to Roman society triggered by the changing climate – food shortages, droughts, and the increased presence of rats, mosquitoes, and other pests. It is possible that climate-induced stress could have started and/or worsened a disease outbreak there in any number of ways – causing animal and human population changes, encouraging conflict or migration, or increasing overall biological stress on populations (Metcalfe, 2024). In effect, "when you have rapid climate change,... it displaces ecosystems, and it destabilizes societies" (Zonneveld et al., 2024).

In their time, Roman systems for everything from sewage to roads were some of the most advanced in history. However, climate and disease were still able to overwhelm many systems. This highlights a risk of treating climate change as a narrow, often dismal topic. It makes ever less sense to think about our systems for healthcare, housing, food, disaster relief, and migration without considering climate change. It doesn't take all that much to bring any one system to the breaking point. As these dominoes fall, we should expect the pressures driving large numbers of human beings to risk migration to intensify rapidly.

A Force Multiplier

In Part I, we described what happens when escaping climate devastation becomes a luxury, but what about the kind of escape you attempt *at all costs?* As climate change multiplies and amplifies existing breakdowns, we should expect more people to attempt to cross borders, no matter the obstacles. We should *also* expect borders to become harder to cross, as long as we continue to focus on symptoms, argues former Costa Rican President Carlos Alvarado-Quesada (Alvarado-Quesada, 2024). Alvarado-Quesada emphasizes the "striking difference between the scale of the resources dedicated to border security and those used to support the implementation, in collaboration with Latin American countries, of long-term structural solutions" (Alvarado-Quesada, 2024).

Unless we change course on climate, we can expect more migration from more places, as conditions become unlivable in much of the world. Long before national borders existed, when environmental pressures grew too great, human beings picked up and moved. Today, no matter how much countries fortify borders, many brave dangerous journeys when circumstances worsen. Pressures to move can outweigh the risks of perilous journeys, border fortifications, lack of work authorization, threats of deportation, and the challenges of survival in a new place.

Though floods, famines, political repression, and war have long been with us, a major new force multiplier now compounds and increases the frequency of the disasters that spur migration. Climate change intensifies the pressures that lead people to pick up and leave.

Dr. Erica Bower served as a climate change and disaster displacement specialist at the UN Office of the High Commissioner for Refugees; she studies mobility in the face of climate change. She notes: "In the 'dry corridor' of Central America, for example, climate change extremes such as droughts may hinder crop production. Without a consistent source of food or income, a farmer may seek other livelihood opportunities in a nearby city or further north" (Jordan, 2021).

In a 2021 discussion at Stanford University, Bower explained how climate change can worsen both economic insecurity and political instability. "When combined with poverty or violence, a drought may make the perilous journey north seem to be a more promising adaptation or survival strategy" (Jordan, 2021). In effect, climate serves as a migration force multiplier, when life in hotter, poorer countries becomes increasingly unlivable.

Over 3 billion people live in places highly vulnerable to climate change, mostly in the Global South (IPCC, 2023). Some of this vulnerability is natural – living along a coast, or in areas near sea level – but worsens as waters rise and ecosystems supporting plant, animal, and human life deteriorate. "We have removed land cover, deforested, and overexploited natural resources. Globally, less than 15% of the land, 21% of the freshwater and 8% of the ocean are protected areas" (IPCC, 2023). Vulnerable areas often lack funds to mitigate climate change.

Widening Displacement

By 2050, the Intergovernmental Panel on Climate Change (IPCC) estimates, over one billion people could be exposed to coast-specific climate hazards, including increasingly extreme weather. This could force tens to hundreds of millions of people to leave their homes, either seasonally or permanently, in the decades to come (IPCC, 2022). Combine these trends with pollution and waning biodiversity, and it becomes much harder for communities to respond to climate change's effects.

For every person who moves, many others face pressures that make it impossible for them to pick up and leave, despite uninhabitable conditions (Zickgraf, 2023). Even so, "circumstances at home" now deteriorate more rapidly in more places than at any time in history.

In 2023, disasters led to over 30 million internally displaced movements and 7.6 million internally displaced persons (IDMC – Internal Displacement Monitoring Center, 2024).[2] The nature of the disaster, and stressor, varies regionally. In 2023, in East Asia and the Pacific, cyclones, floods, and storms displaced the most people. In South Asia, earthquakes, storms, and floods accounted for the most displacement. In Sub-Saharan Africa, flooding and Cyclone Freddy had the greatest impact (IDMC, 2024). The Middle East and North Africa region reported their highest-ever disaster displacements, driven largely by earthquakes and floods. In Europe, Central Asia, and Asia Minor, the earthquakes in Turkey, wildfires, storms, and floods caused disaster displacements. The disaster displacement numbers in the Americas were mostly due to severe storms. Fig. 3 gives a quick snapshot of how the 2023 disasters displaced people in each region.

Disproportionate Impact

As Fig. 3 shows, climate change disproportionately displaces people in the Global South. The imbalance applies to health impacts too: unsurprisingly, "[t]he people [in the developing world] that did the least to contribute to CO_2 emissions are bearing the brunt of the health impacts of climate change" (Malaria No More, 2023).

Vulnerable populations in the Global North, too, face increasing threats. Behavioral scientist Gabrielle Wong-Parodi observes: "We are seeing some evidence that people who feel more impacted by wildfires and ... smoke are more likely to intend to move to a new state within the U.S. or even out of the country" (Jordan, 2021).

The developing country of Bangladesh might be ground zero for rising waters. Many countries around the world face unprecedented floods and other natural

---

[2]The internal displacements figure refers to the number of forced movements of people within the borders of their country recorded during the year. This helps capture repeated and multiple movements. While displacement from conflict and disaster are captured in separate datasets, they can influence and amplify each other's effects.

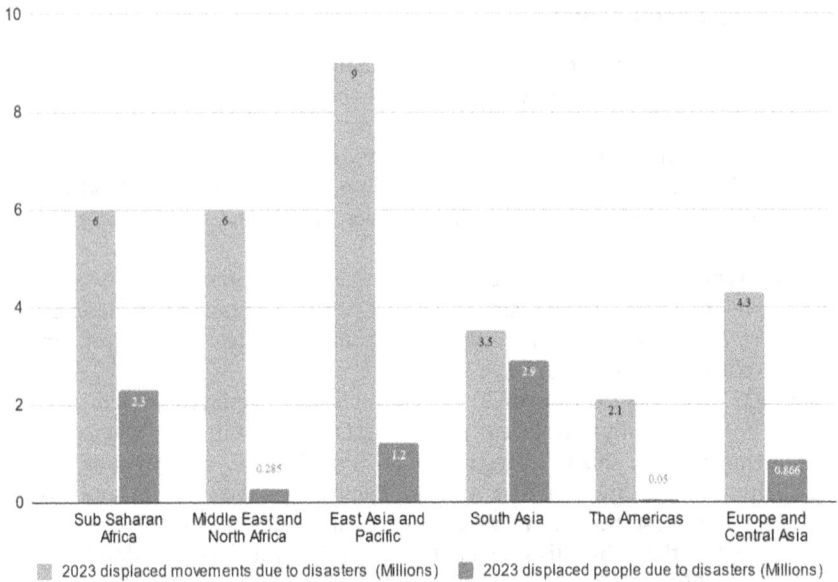

Fig. 3.   2023 Disaster Displacements by Region. *Source:* The authors, adapted from IDMC – Internal Displacement Monitoring Center, 2024.

disasters; at approximately seven feet above sea level (NRDC, 2018), Bangladesh lies fully exposed. Tens and sometimes hundreds of thousands must relocate when the waters rise. If nothing changes, millions (Karim, 2021) will be forced to flee rising seas there. According to Earth.Org, "the UN predicts that over the next decade, about 17% of Bangladeshi would need to be relocated if global warming persists at the present rate" (Ho, 2022).

Bangladesh faces more than just flood waters rising with climate change. Its capital, Dhaka, deals with massive blackouts – including one in 2023 (Paul & Varadhan, 2023) that disrupted everything from safe living environments to crucial irrigation systems during a major heat wave. Bangladesh is home to about half as many people as live in the United States, on about 1.5% of the landmass. It is also one of the poorest countries in the world by per capita gross domestic product (GDP).

Vanuatu and The Marshall Islands are at the other end of the population spectrum. Vanuatu has fewer than 400,000 people spread across the South Pacific, while the Marshall Islands have fewer than 50,000 people dispersed across a part of the Pacific Ocean approximately the size of Mexico. Yet rapidly rising sea levels, sometimes combined with drought, have made life untenable for many residents (Bittle, 2023; Kolbert, 2024).

Just before COP28, the Marshall Islands presented a climate adaptation plan to the United Nations, asking for $35 billion from developed countries to protect their low-lying islands and water supplies (Bittle, 2023). Even with this support, many residents would probably have to migrate within the archipelago, or to the United States, as climate impacts continue. Under a best-case scenario, with immediate action limiting global warming, the Marshall Islands will experience almost two feet of sea-level rise over the next 75 years. "The worst case scenario predicts more than six feet of sea-level rise by 2150. Many islands would disappear into the Pacific. Jobod Silk, a youth climate representative from the Marshall Islands who conducted community interviews for the adaptation plan, commented: 'I hope that we remain on our land, that we remain sovereign, and that we're never labeled as climate change refugees'" (Bittle, 2023).

For its part, Vanuatu initiated proceedings in The International Court of Justice (ICJ) in 2024 to establish that countries have legal and moral obligations to prevent climate disasters, and should face consequences if they don't honor their obligations (Kolbert, 2024). ICJ "proceedings could establish that addressing climate change is a binding legal responsibility.... But for Vanuatu, even a victory won't help all that much" (Kolbert, 2024). The nation is so vulnerable to climate change impacts that it has already had to relocate six villages in the face of rising sea levels. Dozens of others may follow. "Climate displacement of populations is our future.... That's the reality" (Kolbert, 2024).

Bangladesh, Vanuatu, and the Marshall Islands may be bellwethers, but they aren't outliers. The World Bank projects that 216 million people will have to relocate within their countries by 2050, with the potential to destabilize communities, economies, and political systems around the world (World Bank, 2021). That estimate includes only internal climate refugees *within* countries; projections may wildly underestimate the risks past climate tipping points. The International Environmental Partnership predicts that climate change and the natural disasters it worsens could displace 1.2 *billion* people by 2050 (McAllister, 2024).

Disparate Energy Use

A few industries and practices produce the bulk of carbon emissions.[3] People living in a few countries generate per capita emissions wildly disproportionate to what the rest of the world generates. These countries include oil-producing nations, small island nations, and large Western countries outside the EU, like the United States, Canada, and Australia.[4]

---

[3] For detail by industry, please see: https://edgar.jrc.ec.europa.eu/report_2023

[4] Countries producing more than 14 annual tons of carbon per capita include Qatar, the United Arab Emirates, Bahrain, Kuwait, Brunei, Trinidad and Tobago, Saudi Arabia, New Caledonia, Oman, Australia, the United States, Sint Maarten (Dutch part), Canada, the Faroe Islands, and Kazakhstan (Global Carbon Budget, 2023). https://ourworldindata.org/grapher/co-emissions-per-capita?tab5table

The largest contributors to carbon footprint may soon include populous, fast-industrializing countries as well. There are approximately six billion people in the developing world. As they increase their standards of living, they use more energy (CGEP, 2019). Within the next 15 years, developing countries will use two-thirds of global energy, up from 57% in 2017 (CGEP, 2019). China uses the most energy currently, but India's energy needs are projected to grow the fastest, followed by African and other non-OECD Asian countries. The industrial sector, in developing economies, is expected to demand more energy than all sectors combined in developed ones (CGEP, 2019).

As the developed world industrialized, it used fossil fuels and eliminated biodiversity freely. This raises tough questions for economies developing now. For example, Guyana is expected to extract 150 billion dollars' worth of oil and gas over the next 20 years, releasing billions of tons of carbon emissions into the atmosphere. In a BBC interview, reporter Stephen Sankur questioned whether, given its carbon impact, Guyana should be proceeding with this extraction. Guyana's president Irfaan Ali responded that "the world, in the last 50 years, has lost 65% of all its biodiversity. We have kept our biodiversity.... Guyana has a forest, forever, that is the size of England and Scotland combined. A forest that stores 19.5 gigatons of carbon, a forest that we have kept alive ... [t]hat you enjoy, that the world enjoys, that you don't pay us for, that you don't value, that you don't see a value in, that the people of Guyana have kept alive. Are you valuing it? Are you ready to pay for it?" (Velez, 2024).

No One's Coming to Save Us

We're heading for hunger, displacement, and disease on an unprecedented scale, and climate change serves as a force multiplier. What can we do? Part III of this book offers an answer to this question. Before we get there, it's important to understand what's keeping us from making progress. We also need to comprehend why a fundamental shift is needed if we are to avoid a future that makes today's crises look mild by comparison.

It's not that no one's trying. In 2024, for the first time, the United Nations Secretary-General António Guterres called on governments, public relations (PR) firms, and advertising agencies to ban advertisements for products that require fossil fuels and the companies that extract those fuels. More specifically, he asked advertising and PR companies to "stop acting as enablers to planetary destruction," and for governments to ban advertising from fossil fuel companies. So far the cities of Edinburgh, Amsterdam, and Sydney have taken up his call – banning all television advertising for fossil fuel companies, gas-powered cars, airlines, and cruise ships (Guterres, 2024).

But does banning ads solve the problem? If you're going to prohibit ads from fossil fuel companies, why not also regulate the banks that continue to invest in them? What applies to ad agencies and PR firms could be applied to fossil fuel companies themselves, and industries like agriculture, fashion, transportation, or buildings, that continue to generate massive emissions (in that order) (*The World's Most Polluting Industries*, 2023).

The EU has made measurable progress in reducing the emissions of key industries (Crippa et al., 2023). To expand such progress, governments and multinational corporations can play a useful role, but dare we pin our hopes on large, top-down organizations to do the job? In the coming chapters, we'll show how extensively governments and multinationals depend on large global consulting firms to guide their climate transformations. These same consulting firms make their bread and butter from the industries governments regulate. The fox is guarding the henhouse.

Sebastian Groh, the energy innovator quoted earlier, argues we can't afford to hope that someone out there will safeguard our future for us. When we hope for some "Google of climate change" we risk it all on the wrong bet. "We cannot just bet that someone will save us, the way they would in a Hollywood movie. The miracle happens and then the world is rescued,... [and we are passive observers] hoping that this climate change Google shows up" (Crawford & Plavin-Masterman, 2024b). Groh continues, "If we observe what is happening right now in terms of where the money goes, who receives the investment, it's exactly this that the world is betting on right now. And I think this is very, very risky. So we're betting on the superhero, the Hollywood hero coming in and saving all of us at the last minute. And we're hoping that superhero understands our problem" (Crawford & Plavin-Masterman, 2024b).

It's on us. We must create new systems responsive to our needs. To do so is all the more pressing when our reigning economic institutions focus on another priority. Many of them adhere to an extreme ideology called "shareholder primacy." According to this doctrine, when those running a company worry about *any* value besides stock price, they betray their doctrinal responsibility. The consequences of this approach have been anything but theoretical, as we'll show in the next chapter.

Chapter 7

Markets Serve Whom?

Look at Those Quarterly Returns

As the hunt for "efficiency" came to dominate much of our economy, its proponents squeezed the responsiveness from industry after industry, with the results we described in Part I.

How did we get here?

As it became common for large numbers of people to own a company through shares listed on public stock exchanges, more and more companies hired professional managers to run them. Whose interests did those professional managers represent? Those who hold a stake in what a company does (its "stakeholders") arguably include its customers, employees, and owners. They also include members of the community in which the company operates and those impacted by what it produces or by side effects (such as pollution) of doing so.

In 1970, economist Milton Friedman wrote a New York Times piece called "A Friedman Doctrine – The Social Responsibility of Business Is to Increase Its Profits" (Friedman, 1970). Friedman asserted that public corporations' *only goal* should be to advance their owners' interests – generally by making them money. Friedman argued that if professional managers did anything *besides* maximize shareholder value, they were corporate "agents" imposing inefficiencies in the form of "agency costs" on shareholders and society (Jensen & Meckling, 1976).

Shareholder primacy has a neat logic. It gives companies a single goal that sounds logical – reward the owners. Jack Welch, when he led General Electric, implemented Friedman's ideology at scale. "Welch was motivated by an unrelenting desire to drive GE's share [stock] price ever-higher.... He did it with dealmaking. GE made nearly 1,000 acquisitions during Welch's tenure, spending ... \$130 billion buying up companies.... GE [also] sold some 408 businesses for about \$10.6 billion..." (Gelles, 2022a).

A laser focus on share price led Welch to move away from what GE had been known for – making quality appliances and other products. Instead, "the model Jack had was really the Pac-Man model," said Beth Comstock, a longtime GE marketing executive. "Just eat up companies. Acquire growth" (Gelles, 2022a). Welch has long been considered a business "genius" (Brown, 2017; Cohan, 2022).

One Size Fits None, 57–64
Copyright © 2025 Alejandro Juárez Crawford and Miriam Plavin-Masterman
Published under exclusive licence by Emerald Publishing Limited
doi:10.1108/978-1-83608-660-420251008

Yet he grew General Electric's market capitalization from "$14 billion to $400 billion through a very specific kind of financial deception where General Electric would move things around – laying people off, buying new companies, selling old companies and getting into new industries – to match analyst expectations and make his earnings" (Zitron, 2024d).

Welch and GE pioneered obscuring an investment (which markets punish), behind an announcement of layoffs (which markets reward). Previously, many companies turned to layoffs only as a last resort. A company's talent and culture – its labor – gave it an edge in engineering, producing, or marketing quality products. Welch saw labor as a cost to be managed, not an asset in which to invest. He laid off employees as a strategy for increasing profits and rewarded top executives for following suit (Evans, 2023).

Welch showed the short-term power of prioritizing returns to shareholders above investing in research and development (R&D) for *future* returns (Gelles, 2022a). Longer-term value often hinges on investments in R&D along with building a first-rate culture; developing human capacity; nurturing supply chain partners; and fostering relationships with the surrounding community. Yet why bother with building and delivering value to people, when share price can be hiked through manipulation?

Absolute Value

Friedman's doctrine is seductively simple and absolute. A business has one quantifiable goal – to raise value for the shareholder. Stock price gains become the only measure of progress that matters, and executives can justify any action in pursuit of them. Whatever fails to maximize stock price, and do it now, cheats the shareholder. To focus on anything else comes to be seen as suspect and – before long – subject to challenge via shareholder lawsuits.

Such absolutism actively justifies practices that might otherwise have seemed objectionable, instead making them seem necessary. Layoffs, downsizing? Of course, because ... shareholder value. Reduce health or retirement benefits? Same thing. Executive salaries mushrooming out of proportion to those of workers? Well, duh. Stop investing in what the business was good at, say, engineering planes? Look at the stock price! Buy up businesses with debt and strip-mine them? Shareholder value. This simple, all-encompassing paradigm created the moral rationale for the rise of the one-size-fits-all models and pursuit of hockey stick growth we've described. Shareholder primacy furnishes defenses against lawsuits, provides public relations cover, and justifies extensive lobbying against would-be regulators.

Corrective paradigms like stakeholder models, environment, social, and governance (ESG) frameworks, or newer models like doughnut economics, garner significant attention.[1] Some commentators contend that these paradigms actively

---

[1]Doughnut economics proposes that the economy thrives when it exceeds social requirements but stops short of planetary boundaries (Doughnut Economics Action Lab, n.d.).

threaten shareholder primacy's dominance, but they remain outliers in practice. In some cases, they may even function to dress up or soften the image of companies that continue, in practice, to be run according to shareholder primacy.

Shareholder primacy remains the dominant paradigm in the financial community and much of the business world. It is coded into practices for valuing and managing both businesses and economies. It governs how we measure success even as more conventional kinds of value get destroyed before our eyes. For many, it remains the overriding goal Friedman hoped it would become, even when managers pursuing it starve future investment, eviscerate corporate cultures, or hollow out legendary competencies.

A lack of investment in such value-generating activities can be shortsighted in the long run. We wake up one day to news stories about panels falling off airplanes produced by a once-legendary aerospace manufacturer. Then we learn that for decades Boeing applied Welch's model, outsourcing production and cutting costs to jack up stock price. In parallel, the company pulled back investment in its legendary engineering culture and stripped out its capacity to make planes itself (a value considered trivial next to share price) (Surowiecki, 2024).

You Have One Job

Recent generations of leaders, trained in business schools, law schools, and economics departments, have been taught shareholder value as an ideology (Starkey et al., 2025; Stout, 2012). If professors teach students that their job is to maximize shareholder value, and that share price increases demonstrate greater efficiency, we should expect students to focus narrowly on share price. The same professors then write cases retroactively validating the practice. Meanwhile the business press writes glowing books, profiles, and articles about executives like Welch, who have enshrined it as the governing dogma of their companies.

Today, shareholder primacy dominates companies founded to generate other kinds of value. In Google's case, that meant making the world's information more accessible. The company got on the map and then became synonymous with search after transforming the relevance of results. Then that focus shifted, at least according to veteran Google Search engineer Ben Gomes. In 2019, while serving as head of search for the company, Gomes expressed concern that search was "getting too close to the money." He ended his email by saying that he was "concerned that growth is all that Google was thinking about" (Zitron, 2024a). Tech writer Ed Zitron argues that the growth-at-all-costs mindset to which Gomes objected led Google to lose its focus on search excellence. Since then, he argues, "Google Search has dramatically declined, with the numerous core search updates allegedly made to improve the quality of results having an adverse effect, increasing the prevalence of spammy, search engine optimized content" (Zitron, 2024b).

Google, Zitron argues, is no outlier. Focusing on growth, at the expense of building products that respond to our needs, is hollowing out our economy. Zitron describes an "illogical, product-destroying [executive] mindset that turns the products you love into torturous, frustrating quasi-tools that require you to fight the company's intentions to get the service you want" (Zitron, 2024g). Corporate coach B. Lorraine Smith takes this further. She quotes Google's earnings call at the end of 2023, which promoted a "focus on organizational efficiency and structure and 'removing layers', a slower pace of hiring, and headcount down year-on-year." She translates: "that vague word salad suggests that Google is doubling down on profitability by cutting costs, laying off staff, and pouring money into AI – creating a self-reinforcing cycle of over-consumption that is degrading human and ecological wellness" (Smith, 2024).

After a company enshrines shareholder primacy, any goal beyond stock price distracts from the company's purpose. "Returns to shareholders, as measured by stock price, is the main way we define and measure corporate performance, structure executive pay, and think about the role of corporate directors" (Samuelson, 2022). In large tech firms like Meta, Microsoft, and Google parent Alphabet, stock prices rise even as core products stagnate. And as these companies rush to add AI throughout their platforms, they "proliferate unprofitable, unsustainable tech that takes water from the desert and strains our power grids to produce deeply mediocre outcomes based on incredibly vague promises" (Zitron, 2024c). This makes sense when a dollar spent on making the system responsive is a dollar that doesn't go to short-term stock price inflation.

Google's diminishing responsiveness illustrates how the pursuit of share price eclipses other values. The company's stated purpose is to organize the world's information and (as we noted) make it universally accessible and useful. When Google offered shares to the public in 2004, the accompanying letter noted the tension between that purpose and a structure that committed the company to focus narrowly on the interests of shareholders. The letter highlighted the risk that shareholder primacy could divert Google from the value it was built to create: "the standard structure of public ownership may jeopardize the independence and focused objectivity that have been most important in Google's past success and that we consider most fundamental for its future" (Smith, 2024).

Businesses can escape this false dichotomy. Capital is a tool, not an end in itself. Entrepreneurs and others need resources to build solutions before those solutions can pay for themselves. Returns compensate capital providers for risking their resources on them. Those returns make it possible to risk capital on experiments that might fail. The more audacious the experiment, the more risk – so the greater the needed returns. To take a simple example, if you risk capital on 10 experiments, each of which has a 10% chance of succeeding, then you need the one that succeeds (on average) to return more than 10 times the capital you risked.

When returns become the only goal – when the doctrine of shareholder primacy eclipses capital's function in funding better solutions – we get the kinds of cattle-class economies we described in Part I of this book. A singular focus on returns distorts decisions and outcomes. The high priests of primacy would have us think that people build what we need when they're motivated to increase profits, and through them, share price. But as examples like those of GE, Boeing, and Alphabet show, a *narrow* focus on increasing profits leads managers to *neglect* the activities that build economic value. Jacking up short-term stock prices often interferes with value creation. Shareholder primacy ignores the many reasons people pursue excellence in their work and through what they build. It takes a purpose that responds to people's needs (making information accessible) and subordinates it to a tool (generating returns).

Brilliant

The shareholder primacy model rewards CEOs for managing metrics to make their companies look like they are always growing. The other side of this coin is that companies select and compensate executives for something other than knowing how to generate value through the core business (Gelles, 2022b; Zitron, 2024d). "Welch gave birth to . . . the culture of the overpaid and ever-distant chief executive, a con artist that moves numbers around to make rich people happy, one that will never – and maybe never has – participated in the value exchange that makes them rich, all while lacking any fundamental appreciation of or respect for labor, all while demanding complete fealty from it. These people have now mentored themselves across generations of business people, hiring them and training others to be like them" (Zitron, 2024c).

At GE, Welch trained generations of business leaders, some of whom went on to run Home Depot, Chrysler, and Boeing, where they mostly failed. "A lot of GE leaders were thought to be business geniuses," said Bill George, the former CEO of Medtronic. "But they were just cost cutters. And you can't cost cut your way to prosperity" (Gelles, 2022b). Welch's acolytes at Boeing, former CEOs Stonecipher, and then Calhoun, adopted a shareholder primacy mindset that neglected investment in engineering excellence or research and development (Surowiecki, 2024).

We continue to reward and incentivize this approach. Pay for executives keeps rising, without improvements in company performance. Studies show that "large companies' performance, including stock price, have [*sic*] almost no relation to how much the companies paid their CEOs. . . . You look at the highest-paid CEOs versus the lower-paid ones, then look at returns to shareholders 10 years later. You just get no relationship at all between more pay and higher return to shareholders – and that is assuming that all anyone cares about with CEO pay is the return to shareholders" (Kreidler, 2024).

The Washington, D.C.-based Economic Policy Institute (EPI) has published research showing that from 1978–2021, CEOs at the top 350 publicly traded firms in the United States saw their average compensation package grow by 1,460%, compared to an approximately 18% gain for typical US workers, *adjusted for inflation*. CEO pay rose even faster than the S&P 500 index of leading firms' stock performance over the same period (Kreidler, 2024).

"Fat" Trimming

As a percentage of corporate assets, employee wages have been in free fall, dropping by almost half over the last five decades – from 21% of assets in 1972 to 11% in 2017 (Samuelson, 2022). Lower wages might sound good if you look at employees as a cost, a drag on the boat. But thriving economies depend upon a broad base of spending power. When shareholder primacy encourages companies to minimize investment in people and treats that investment as a form of waste, it removes value *from* the economy. Past a certain point, gains in the form of executive compensation may stay largely out of circulation. While stock market gains can strengthen retirement portfolios, stock portfolios are far more narrowly disseminated than wages. As wages drop, cheap, automated products and services become what folks in cattle class can afford. According to University of Massachusetts Public Policy professor Lenore Palladino:

> Total wages have been below 15% of assets every year since 2001.... Meanwhile, payments to shareholders have doubled as a percentage of assets, from 1.7% in 1972 to 3.5% in 2017. These shifts are consistent with a story of rising shareholder power and declining employee bargaining power. (Palladino, 2019)

Even when discussing a corporation's ESG responsibilities, whenever trade-offs emerge, the shareholder takes priority. Stock price obsession and short-termism are intertwined: a corporate board's definition of "long-term" today is about *3 years*. Companies regularly highlight ESG commitments, but the market still rewards actions like laying off workers or replacing full-time workers with contractors, while punishing companies that invest in their employees. In 2011, when Google announced its intention to create 1,600 new jobs, the stock price fell 5% in less than a day. When in 2023, by contrast, the company laid off workers, it employed the language with which we opened Chapter 3: "A number of our teams made changes to become more efficient and work better, and to align their resources to their biggest product priorities." This is shareholder primacy in effect. Even when business is booming, lay off workers to chase stock price increases.

Beyond the tech sector, an economy dominated by shareholder primacy punishes companies that diverge from such practices. In 2015, Walmart announced a planned minimum wage increase, along with increased worker training and the use of technology to improve jobs and productivity. In response, investors punished the company, effecting a 20-billion-dollar loss in stock value. American Airlines was similarly penalized in 2017 after announcing raises for its employees after a bankruptcy-driven reorganization (Samuelson, 2022).

Inflated CEO pay creates perverse incentives, since most CEO paychecks consist largely of current or future stock awards. Throughout the 2010s, 93% of all profits of companies in the S&P 500 were returned to shareholders via stock buybacks and dividends (Lala & Palladino, 2020).[2] When companies buy back their shares, they manage fewer publicly available shares and also increase the value of the remaining shares. CEOs direct their companies to buy back shares instead of investing in processes, paying employees, or improving customer service, because stock buybacks increase executive pay. This is what boards, CFOs, and CEOs are now incentivized to do. When the Biden administration tried to revive the United States' semiconductor industry by subsidizing new domestic chip factories, these efforts were "endangered by the increasing likelihood that those subsidies [would] enrich big shareholders and CEOs rather than strengthen the country's semiconductor industrial base.... [N]early $30 billion in federal CHIPS grants [were] awarded, with the grants going to 11 semiconductor producers. But most of these producers ... spent billions buying back their shares of stock to raise their share prices. And every dollar the semiconductor producers spend on buybacks is a dollar not spent on innovation for long-term competitiveness" (Reich, 2024).

Giant CEO paydays increase pay for those a level or two below the CEO as well (Kreidler, 2024). Executive pay skyrockets even while companies fail to perform any better, even for their shareholders. Nice work if you can get it. In the past few years, for the top 1% in the United States, wealth grew by over $11.5 trillion versus $1.6 trillion for the bottom 50% (Samuelson, 2022).

Shareholder primacy functions as a kind of flywheel driving income inequality, since a relentless focus on stock price benefits those owning stocks (Samuelson, 2022). In 2024, the wealth of the top 1% of Americans hit $44.6 trillion, driven mostly by investments. More specifically, "the top 10% of Americans own 87% of individually held stocks and mutual funds. The top 1% own half of all individually held stocks" (Frank, 2024). As Judy Samuelson, executive director of the Aspen Institute's Business and Society program has observed in testimony before Congress: "Most stocks are owned by the wealthy – the biggest share of stocks are owned by people who are already extremely wealthy" (Samuelson, 2022). Between 1978 and 2021, the top 0.1% of US earners' income growth was 385% (Kreidler, 2024).

You Have It or You Don't

There are other ways to run corporations, in which, for example, employees across all levels have ownership shares, build wealth, and are invested in company success. As entrepreneur Margaret Heffernan emphasized in her 2015 TED Talk: "Most organizations have spent the past 50 years or more adhering to pecking orders in which success is achieved by picking the superstars, the brightest men or ... women in the room,.... giving them all the resources and all the power..." (Heffernan, 2015). This, Heffernan argues, leads to "aggression, dysfunction and waste." Time for a new plan: "If the only way the productive can be successful is

---

[2] A practice disallowed in the United States until 1982 (Reich, 2024).

by suppressing the productivity of the rest, then we ... need to find a better way to work and [a] richer way to live" (Heffernan, 2015).

Indiana University social psychologist Mary Murphy makes a similar point in her book *Cultures of Growth*. Picking superstars, she argues, delivers the message that "people's abilities are unchangeable, or fixed. People either 'have it' or they don't, and there's little anyone can do to change this" (Murphy, 2024, pp. 8–9). Increasingly, this belief characterizes the move to replace the "median worker" altogether or reduce her role to a limited function alongside what the algorithm does.

As the crises we have described accelerate, there isn't much time left to change course. Unfortunately, as we'll see in the next chapter, the industry that advises leaders of both companies and governments is taking us in the wrong direction fast.

Chapter 8

All the Running You Can Do, to Keep in the Same Place

Alice looked 'round her in great surprise. 'Why, I do believe we've been under this tree the whole time! Everything's just as it was!'

'Of course it is,' said the Queen, 'what would you have it?'

'Well, in our country,' said Alice, still panting a little, 'you'd generally get to somewhere else – if you ran very fast for a long time, as we've been doing.'

'A slow sort of country!' said the Queen. 'Now, here, you see, it takes all the running you can do, to keep in the same place. If you want to get somewhere else, you must run at least twice as fast as that!' – Alice in Wonderland (Carroll, 2010, p. 19)

Faster, Faster

Companies and governments regularly announce their leadership in the green transformation. Yet overall we fail to gain ground. We run faster and faster but end up in the same place.

Majorities the world over *recognize* we face a crisis, but live and work within systems failing broadly to respond to it. How does such systematic distortion happen? What widens the gap between what serves most of us and what our economy functions to do? How do cattle class models spread like a virus across industries and regions? Why do we double down on fossil fuels as life becomes increasingly untenable for more of us?

Hint: it's not that corporate leaders magically move in lockstep. It's not even just shared education in the shareholder primacy doctrine. There's an industry for this, one that brings well-honed tools for spreading unresponsive models.

Many of us harbor the illusion that executives and elected officials run our largest organizations, but over the last 50 years, leaders increasingly began hiring

One Size Fits None, 65–75

Copyright © 2025 Alejandro Juárez Crawford and Miriam Plavin-Masterman
Published under exclusive licence by Emerald Publishing Limited
doi:10.1108/978-1-83608-660-420251009

large global consulting firms to do the heavy lifting for them. In the process, as Mariana Mazzucato and Rosie Collington describe in *The Big Con,* many companies and governments hollowed out their capacity or let it atrophy. Top consulting firms replicate many of the same approaches across companies, industries, governments, and economies. Guess what? These approaches often pursue the efficiencies and one-size-fits-all scalability of cattle class models.

Workin' Both Sides

Globally, a few consulting firms set strategies *both* for fossil fuel companies *and* for responding to climate change. Even as top consultancies announce commitments to minimizing carbon and solving other crises, those same advisory firms help clients implement models that make progress elusive.

The authors are not predisposed to scapegoat consulting as a function. If anything, both of us value key tools in the consultant's kit. We teach in business programs and have worked as management consultants. Yet as we researched for this book, we learned a great deal about the role of the consulting industry in spreading unresponsive systems.

Let's begin with an example involving the leading consultancy McKinsey, drawn from *The Big Con,* Mazzucato and Collington's critique of the global management consulting industry. "In 2021 [Australia] contracted McKinsey to help develop the Long-Term Emissions Reduction Plan. The report sets out a strategy for reaching net zero by 2050, using modeling carried out by McKinsey as part of an AUD$6 million contract" (Mazzucato & Collington, 2023, p. 190).

Australia, Mazzucato and Collington note, ranks 14th among global countries for carbon emissions, ahead of the United States, China, and Saudi Arabia. Even if Australia were to follow its strategy, McKinsey projected, the country would "fall 215 metric tons short of reaching ... an 85% reduction [in emissions] by 2050" (Mazzucato & Collington, 2023, p. 191). The remaining 15% reduction in emissions would hinge on "further technology breakthroughs emerging from some unspecified place..., at some unspecified point in time before 2050" (Mazzucato & Collington, 2023, p. 224).

Why such modest targets? McKinsey has the resources to create a strategy that pays more than lip service to a goal. The firm is famous for advising executives to take no prisoners to grow and dominate markets. Yet here, its recommendations would maintain business as usual for some of Australia's worst-offender export industries, such as natural gas and aluminum. Though in theory, Australia's coal sector would shrink by 51%, emissions from the gas industry would be 13% *higher* in 2050 than they are today (Mazzucato & Collington, 2023, pp. 224–225).

Australia's coal and natural gas exports have roughly three times the carbon footprint of the country's total domestic emissions. Aluminum contributes greatly to CO_2 emissions, but McKinsey's plan focused elsewhere, including projections for what would happen if farmers planted more trees: "10–20 percent of the reduction would come from 'offsets' achieved through ... questionable methods, including abatement payments to landowners to incentivize them to manage their soils and plant trees that temporarily store carbon" (Mazzucato & Collington, 2023, pp. 224–225).

Offset programs have minimal net impact. But, sure, "plant more trees" – this from a firm famous for the analytical chops it can bring to bear when it wishes.

Bread and Butter

For Australia, the actions McKinsey recommended were *unlikely to reduce carbon quickly on net*. What's happening here?

According to an investigation by news agency AFP, McKinsey claims to advise on climate progress, but may be highly conflicted in practice (News Wires, 2023). In this, McKinsey is not alone. Along with a handful of other firms – including, but not limited to, top strategy shops like Boston Consulting Group, Bain, and other competitors – McKinsey advises many of the most powerful companies and governments in the world.

McKinsey also serves as a major advisor to COP, the UN's annual global climate Conference of Parties. An investigation by AFP suggests that in 2023, "behind closed doors, the US-based firm has proposed future energy scenarios to the agenda setters of the summit that are at odds with the climate goals it publicly espouses" (News Wires, 2023). In response, the firm emphasized that "sustainability is a mission-critical priority" and stressed pride in the expertise it was able to bring to the conference. "We are proud to be supporting COP28 by providing strategic insight and analysis, and sectoral and technical expertise" (News Wires, 2023).

Yet when it came to recommendations for *action,* McKinsey sang a different tune, "vocally and brazenly calling for lower levels of ambition on oil phase-out at the highest levels within the COP28 presidency," according to "a source who was in the room on confidential discussions with the summit hosts" (News Wires, 2023). AFP obtained the "energy transition narrative" drafted by the consultancy. It proposes just a 50% reduction in oil use by 2050, and "calls for trillions in new oil and gas investment per year from now until then" (News Wires, 2023). Subsequent COPs show little more promise. Even as leaders talk about big reductions in fossil fuels, they keep investing in them as if the party might never end. And the experts advising these leaders on how to sound like they're ready to act with urgency are also the ones developing their plans to do too little, too late (Robinson, 2023).

Why would consultancies that trumpet sustainability publicly continue to give such advice? Let's return to our mini case study on McKinsey, whose client rosters include the world's largest fossil fuel interests. "McKinsey – whose big oil clients range from America's ExxonMobil to Saudi Arabia's state-run Aramco – is one of several consultancies giving free advice to the United Arab Emirates as it hosts the critical [COP] negotiations, which start on November 30 [2023]" (News Wires, 2023). Consultants like McKinsey are notorious for working both sides of the issue, often advising "both the companies that create problems and the governments that are trying to solve them" (Robinson, 2023). The fossil fuel clients are often the ones paying for big consulting contracts; the consultancies know which side their bread is buttered on. Even when big consultancies present their green advice and win contracts with governments to go green, we go faster and faster and get nowhere.

The Call Is Coming From Inside the House

While COP28 and McKinsey provide a stark illustration, similar dynamics now determine the public and private conduct of many of the largest and most influential companies, banks, governments, and other institutions worldwide. The world seems decentralized, but the same few consultancies advise the leading institutions in it, drawing from a common playbook. A huge part of that playbook has always been driving efficiency by cutting "redundancies," or jobs.

For many consultancies, jobs are fat to be trimmed, often while hiking management pay. In his memoir *Rip Off,* former consultant David Craig gives the example of "a manager who had just business-process-reengineered an organization, reducing staff from 36,000 employees to only 16,000, breezily explain[ing] . . . that 'we were just getting rid of the rubbish'" (Craig, 2005, p. 39). This is no isolated anecdote. As *Boondoggle's* Pat Garofalo has observed:

> Advocating for layoffs is a key part of the McKinsey playbook, which it dresses up as a quest for 'efficiency.' A 2013 book on McKinsey said it may be "the single greatest legitimizer of mass layoffs [of] anyone, anywhere, at any time in modern history." As one former McKinsey employee explained, "Even at its best, much of the work is about increasing investors' share of the profits by reducing labor's share." (Garofalo, 2024)

Hello, shareholder primacy. But hold the phone: why would the government of Australia hire consultants using this playbook, when it has no share price to hike? Why hire them to develop a strategy for reducing emissions over the long term, as we've described? For that project, Australia had significant in-house capacity, determined to do the work. The country's national science agency CSIRO even competed with McKinsey for the contract (Mazzucato & Collington, 2023, p. 226).

Cynics argue that executives hire companies like McKinsey to create "the illusion of ambitious climate action," with models intended "to lend the plan credibility" (Mazzucato & Collington, 2023, p. 226). AFP's investigation into COP28 exposed the firm's work, during the global climate conference, to advance or protect fossil fuel interests. According to "a source who took part in COP28 presidency discussions":

> They would give advice at the highest levels that was not in the best interest of the COP president as the leader of a multilateral climate agreement, but in the best interest of the COP president as

the CEO of one of the region's biggest oil and gas companies.
(News Wires, 2023)

The call is coming from inside the house. The companies advising countries on how to reduce emissions are also helping advance the use of fossil fuels at current or increasing rates. Climate change and job loss might seem less terrifying than the killer in a horror film. At least no one's running around in a mask slashing people. But consider the data in this book. How many people's lives will climate change or "efficient" job cuts slash in the next 5 years? We're in a horror film. Climate change is far more dangerous than a knife-wielding killer. Still, we assume the threat is coming from *elsewhere*.

Trust Us

How big is the consulting industry? As of 2021 there were over 2,392,685 "business consulting firms" (Catherine, 2021), with over a third of these based in Europe and more than another third in the United States (large firms keep offices in many countries). In 2024, the industry generated an estimated $1 trillion in revenues (IBIS World, 2024).

Why do firms and governments hire consultancies? For one thing, skilled consultants can help connect knowledge that lives in siloes. For example, one of the authors led an effort for a multi-department organization to draw from each department's local knowledge, and then collaborate strategically. The team helped draw on deep experience within each department to create a strategic plan and align around shared goals. Then it saw that this did not go far enough, because those close to the ground knew about problems the department heads didn't. So the team designed a forum where 600 employees could draw on their experience working with folks in the community to identify needs that *weren't* being met. Guess who had the best insights? People the CEO had never met brought specific problems. They then derived solutions – ones neither department heads nor "C-level" executives had come up with.

Consulting can add real value, beyond walking into a room and dominating discussion with little in-depth knowledge of facts on the ground. In the foregoing instance, the consulting team might have started as a "sage on the stage," but quickly became a "guide on the side" (King, 1993). Yet consultants often remain in the role of sage on the stage. This increases the danger that companies will use consultants' advice to justify *inaction*, as AFP's investigation of McKinsey's role at COP28 suggests. Consultants, for their part, often lack exposure to downside risks from their recommendations. Beyond not being hired for follow-up work, they face few consequences. As *Antifragile* author Nassim Nicholas Taleb writes, "Every opinion maker needs to have 'skin in the game' in the event of harm caused by reliance on his information or opinion.... Pilots should be on the plane" (Taleb, 2013, pp. 497–498). Too often, the consultancy sets the plane's direction but does not fly with it to its destination, let alone land it safely.

The importance, for consultancies' business models, of generating repeat contracts from deep-pocketed clients can also create powerful incentives to protect business as usual. Consulting firms may say they're all about innovation – just look at their websites or recent reports – while using their strategic and analytical credibility to protect incumbent firms. Challenging existing practices often requires new ways of thinking, but consultancies depend upon reusing approaches that have proven powerful before. Top firms hire people who can quickly recognize and solve "cases." Cracking the case means recognizing situations and applying analyses drawn from other situations.

This approach can be effective for eliminating certain kinds of "inefficiencies," justifying layoffs, outsourcing functions, and helping firms dominate their markets. It can help squeeze more juice out of the orange or grow larger oranges, but may be less effective for changing the food system. Today, we're faced with the challenge of reinventing the global economy. The innovation we need requires new ideas, not recycled advice.

The Best and the Brightest

Consultants are trained to draw on time-tested tools to present ideas *commandingly,* organizing chaos into insights that leap from the slide or page. These insights come with an aura of credibility. The consultancy's reputation, along with its published research, suggests that it brings deep wells of knowledge.

After an experienced partner sells the job, the average consulting team at a top strategy shop is staffed by 20-something alumni of elite colleges or recent graduates of top MBA programs. Few such grads bring experience piloting organizations or innovating solutions. They bring relatively limited real-world experience beyond canned case studies, PowerPoint presentations, and spreadsheet analyses. One of the authors remembers telling her late grandmother that she had lined up a consulting job at a well-known, global firm, after completing her MBA. Her grandmother didn't understand what consultants did, so the author explained, "When companies have problems they hire consultants to solve their problems." Her grandmother replied, "Why should they hire you? What do you know?"

Ouch, but Grandma was not wrong. How could consultants like her granddaughter possibly be in a position to tell longtime managers what they should do? Consultancies draw credibility from what organization scholar Mary Murphy calls "cultures of genius" (Murphy, 2024). Such organizational cultures benefit from and perpetuate the myth that a few brilliant people know and can do what the rest of us can't. Shops like Bain, BCG, McKinsey, and their competitors trade on cultures of genius.

Beyond reputation, the consulting toolkit brings ways of conveying ideas that can make smart people who don't understand problems in-depth seem authoritative. Consultants are trained to use "frameworks" – paradigms that allow a whole variety of problems to be analyzed quickly by generalists appearing to derive powerful insights. This can be impressive. It can also become a substitute for deep work by people who go in-depth with the problems. In *Rip Off*, Craig explains how consultancies he worked for used the same pyrotechnics everywhere. "We could take somebody ... off the street, teach them ... simple tricks in a couple of hours and easily charge them out to our clients for more than £7,000 per week" (Craig, 2005, p. 14). Craig describes how this superficial sophistication became a mainstay of the work. He writes of work with "an American consultancy ... the guiding father for many consultancies ... in existence today" (Craig, 2005, p. 39):

> When [we] started a project, they knew that ... estimated savings potential was often based on analysis by totally inexperienced consultants.... [We] got paid whether results were achieved or not. (Craig, 2005, pp. 22–23)

It's worth being skeptical about personal accounts like Craig's; there can be a fine line between muckraking and sensationalizing. But his excoriations raise questions that bear asking about an industry advising all others. The consultant's tool kit can easily become a set of hammers looking for nails to bang into place. An industry that trades on neat frameworks risks bringing neat frameworks to everything. As blogger Michael Roberts observes, "There are now half a million management consultants in the world and they all claim to be able to enter any organization, watch its workers for a short period, and then – using graphs, algorithms, and a jargon that makes quantum physics look like Sesame Street – render it dramatically more efficient, for a fee" (Roberts, 2023).

In the authors' own experience as consultants early in our careers, management consultants often add value by bringing an outside perspective in. As one of us observed on our podcast, *What if Instead?*:

> Consultants are by their nature fish out of water. They come somewhere.... Hopefully bring best practices and help people in an organization get better at something. And then they move on. And I remember thinking when I was a consultant, when I got too comfortable somewhere, it was time for me to go. Actively ... thinking ... I'm too comfortable.... I need to go somewhere else.... I felt like I had more distance to help solve problems if I was a little less familiar with the people that I was helping. (Crawford & Plavin-Masterman, 2024c)

Outsiders can bring this advantage. That said, consultancies can also spread one-size-fits-none models quickly across whole industries. They often function as the "carrier" bringing these models to new industries and wringing the responsiveness out of systems in the name of efficiency, scalability, and profitability.

"Savings" You Can Count

The consulting industry grew dramatically by replicating and adapting cost-cutting playbooks across industries and situations. Consulting teams formulated strategies to justify "downsizing" and planned waves of mergers and acquisitions that removed "redundancies" (people). Other consultancies (and sometimes the same ones) then showed firms how to implement one-size technologies to further reduce costs. Facing objections, executives could say "Don't blame me: Bain or McKinsey showed us that we had to. Just look at this report they gave us." Often, they could point out success derived from locking up markets, growing quarterly returns, and jacking up stock prices. The firms that could afford such consulting were typically incumbents with a vested interest in consolidating market power and resisting "creative destruction."[1]

To sweeten the deal, the labor of all these consultants counts as a temporary cost on company books. We've discussed the role of consultants in recommending and managing layoffs; guess who often then comes in to fill the void? Consultants frequently take on functions previously performed by employees who have been "made redundant" (laid off). Employees working for a firm like Capgemini or one of its competitors often work directly as part of a client organization's team. Though nominally temporary, they do this on an ongoing basis. In day-to-day work interactions, they seem like company employees. But they're not on the client company's books as employees. Employees can prove difficult to get rid of at will and are typically considered a *fixed* cost by accountants.[2]

Even if the consultant has taken on work previously done by employees who have been "downsized" or treated as redundant, the company can stop hiring the consultant at any point. So though consultants take on a significant share of a company's work, they look like a discretionary, strategic expenditure, not an ongoing fixed cost. For consultants, benefits like retirement (and health insurance, in a country like the United States where most people depend on employer-provided health insurance) typically aren't on the client company's books either. They do the *work* of employees while the company bears no responsibility to them as employees – a perfect result from the standpoint of shareholder primacy.

Leading strategy consultancies have played a significant role in spreading shareholder primacy and industry consolidation. Meanwhile, consulting firms that built their reputations around tech implementation, accounting services, or outsourcing – like Accenture, Deloitte, or Capgemini – apply software models to everything, then fill in missing capabilities to replace eliminated roles. These firms convert shareholder primacy, industry consolidation, and one-size-fits-none

---

[1]"Creative destruction refers to the incessant product and process innovation mechanism by which new production units replace outdated ones. It was coined by Joseph Schumpeter (1942), who considered it 'the essential fact about capitalism'" (Caballero, 2008, pp. 1–5).
[2]Employees constitute a yearly recurring expense, which must be deducted from the money that comes in when calculating profits. They count as a cost the company needs to pay in a given period, rather than one that varies with how much it sells.

models from theories into operational realities. With corporate executive pay packages tied to stock price, cattle class models can be trumpeted as success stories and triumphant case studies, even if in the process life gets worse for employees and consumers.

Through this process, life in cattle class became the norm over half a century, as consultancies helped operationalize a set of business theories systematically. After one company in an industry saw share prices soar while short-term costs decreased, these approaches often became competitive necessities. Worse still, industries that seem inefficient under this model face increasing pressure to perform like industries that have already had the responsiveness wrung out of them. As people wielding spreadsheets apply this pressure, they often squeeze out of an industry what it costs to do things well.

Decision Time

Consulting strategies involve more than cost-cutting. They often entail cementing market and regulatory advantages. We call these advantages "unfair" because they raise barriers to competition and block creative destruction. For innovators, every unfair advantage to the incumbent makes the challenger's job harder, tightening the stranglehold on innovation.

Innovators in the developing world often contend with versions of this stranglehold that are built in as a condition of development financing. In Nigeria, Guinea-Bissau, Mexico, and Angola, hiring consultants was written into their *IMF loan agreements* (Craig, 2005, p. 57).

Green innovators in particular must fight an uphill battle against incumbents' market power and regulatory advantages, along with industry dynamics distorted by consolidation. Consolidation compounds the "greenwashing" problem we introduced earlier. Consultants badly want climate business. As Mazzucato and Collington note, "among consultancies large and small, the battle for climate clients has become fierce. Where once environmental considerations were buried within broader 'corporate social responsibility' services, today they are front and center of consultancies' marketing material" (Mazzucato & Collington, 2023, p. 215). Unfortunately, as in the example of Australia's emissions-reduction plan, consultancies often help countries and companies to sound green, or follow a "lite" sustainability policy while buffing their image among consumers and community stakeholders who care about sustainability.

Consultancies do invest in real research on climate change; "their websites are replete with beautifully designed free reports on sustainability issues for every sector, from oil and gas to healthcare, and from government to luxury goods.... Briefing papers have titles such as 'The time for climate action is now' and 'Sustainable finance: it's decision time'" (Mazzucato & Collington, 2023, p. 216). Still, consultancies with big oil among their clients have every institutional incentive to protect those clients' businesses. When you take this into account, Alice's problem in Wonderland – running faster and faster only to end up in the same place – doesn't seem as strange. We expend significant effort on climate, and all the while the fossil economy flourishes. If consultancies can get paid for climate strategy *and* make their fossil fuel clients more money, no one loses! Well, except for the rest of us, when this slows climate transformation and hobbles regulations that could stop bad actors from imposing their costs of doing business onto us.

To Get Somewhere Else

Climate consulting is itself good business – and better if we always need more. Some firms project the global climate change consulting market to be worth over $8 billion by 2028 (Coherent Market Insights, 2021). This will only grow with unsolved climate change.

> Increasing carbon emission is expected to propel growth of the global climate change consulting market over the forecast period.... According to the Global Carbon Project, emissions from fossil fuel and industry are expected to reach 36.81bn tonnes of CO_2 (GtCO$_2$) in 2019, recording an increase of 0.6% from 2018 levels. (Coherent Market Insights, 2021)

While the hunting's good if you're a consultant, the window keeps narrowing to transform our industries away from fossil fuels and seize the massive opportunities involved. To move past fossil fuels requires remaking the way we do things on the ground, and that comes down to the *details*. We need widespread experimentation now at every level of industry, everywhere, to create the models that will replace the way we do things today. Despite the glossy reports, much of the global consulting industry is effectively using the formidable tools at its disposal, and deploying the intensive intellectual labor of so many of our brightest graduates, to forestall this outcome.

There are many small, boutique consultancies all over the world working to move the climate dial. Consultants have developed useful expertise in everything from measuring carbon impact to managing transitions and transformations for high-carbon-footprint areas like electricity and heat, transportation, manufacturing and construction, agriculture, buildings, waste, and shipping and aviation (Ritchie et al., 2020).

Still, the game the top consulting firms play is inherently top-down. Bain & Company founder Bill Bain made his company famous early in its history for *only* working with the top decision-maker at a leading firm in a given industry. While not every firm is as selective, Bain's rule highlights the extent to which big consultancies work for incumbents already at the top. With few exceptions, only large organizations can afford to hire McKinsey, Bain, BCG, or Accenture. Broad-based economic transformation historically begins somewhere very different entirely. As the authors emphasized in an op-ed co-written with cleantech investor and *Climate and Capital* Executive Editor Barclay Palmer:

Top-down solutions appeal to our desire for simple narratives and strong leaders. But they often lack the adaptability to address the needs of different industries, markets, and communities. As five-year plans and the famines that followed have long demonstrated, such top-down solutions promise scale, but often fail – tragically. (Crawford et al., 2023)

The economic transformation we need may only be possible from the "bottom" up. The op-ed continues:

As Cara Kiewel, energy program manager for the Bard MBA in Sustainability, observes, top-down solutions only get us a fraction of the way toward net zero. While more than a third of large firms have committed to hit net-zero goals by 2030, Accenture projects that 93% will fall short if they stay on their current trajectory (Accenture, 2022). (Crawford et al., 2023)

If Kiewel is right, and we need to work from the bottom up, what would we do? Part III of this book answers this question.

It's not the approach to innovation we're taking today.

Chapter 9

Genius!

Unplug the Rest

Today's system for financing innovation relies heavily on anointing "geniuses" and handing them the resources to build what comes next. Unfortunately, those who gain access to venture capital (VC) – not to mention corporate and government capital – tend not to face the problems the rest of us face.

VC enjoys an almost mythic reputation for finding and investing in what has the most potential. This bears a closer look. A typical VC firm raises money from investors, promising high risks with spectacular returns. The VC then turns around and bets this money on startups and growing firms. Economist Michael Shuman observes: "VC funds purchase control of 10–20 businesses, invest heavily in their rapid growth, take a few public, and unplug the rest" (Shuman, 2024).[1]

A few firms dominate the game, investing in startups they deem likely to multiply in value. As Shuman describes, early investors can cash in or "exit" when a startup goes "public" (offers shares for purchase on a stock exchange). Often, investors exit when a large firm acquires the company, buys a major stake in it, or (in a practice that gained popularity in the 2020s) licenses its innovation while hiring its team.[2] Startups that fail to progress toward these attractive exits get, to use Shuman's term, "unplugged."

This model certainly generates results for a few entrepreneurs and for wealthy investors who make early bets on "disruptive technologies." Bet on world-changing

---

[1]Some large firms and governments attempt to borrow from this model through vehicles such as corporate VC and strategic government funds. Various "accelerators" promise to help startups reach the next stage and secure the relevant funding.

[2]In the 2020s, big tech experimented with new mechanisms for acquiring innovations developed by startups. In 2014, Google acquired AI firm DeepMind (Gibbs, 2024). Ten years later, under antitrust scrutiny, the tech giant agreed to pay billions to license the technology of another AI startup, Character.AI. Google used most of the licensing fees to buy out the shareholders, while hiring the founders along with key employees. Microsoft and Amazon have pursued similar strategies for acquiring innovations in ways that compensate founders and investors without acquiring the firms outright (Griffith & Metz, 2024).

One Size Fits None, 77–86

Copyright © 2025 Alejandro Juárez Crawford and Miriam Plavin-Masterman

Published under exclusive licence by Emerald Publishing Limited

doi:10.1108/978-1-83608-660-420251010

innovations, and see which sink or swim! This model has helped launch technologies unheard of a short time ago, that many of us now use throughout our waking hours. It also fuels the hunt for flywheel effects and hockey sticks, that we described in Part I. Scratch a major VC, and chances are they're seeking models that scale like software (Brush, 2024).

When already wealthy venture investors function as gatekeepers for innovation funding, they can cluster resources around a few models and opportunities. Such clustering can enable astounding shifts, from the percentage of young people's lives spent on social media to the amount of new written work authored by large language models. It can also magnify the damage when a bubble bursts. In the meantime, this model often leaves solutions and problem solvers that don't fit the profile struggling to access capital.

Synchronized Swimmers

Why would VCs cluster?

In early 2023 VC investing dropped by about half across all stages of companies (Teare, 2023). To the extent that VC recovered in 2024, it depended on a few AI investments. VC has long followed the latest tech waves. In the early 2000s, when the dot-com bubble burst, investment dropped off a cliff. Investment by US VCs fell by 65% from 2000 to 2001 (Adams, 2002). While it stands to reason that venture investing would chase new opportunities in tech, VC doesn't just follow the cycle of boom and bust, it often leads it. A charitable interpretation would be that leading VCs expertly identify good risks early and then get out at the right point. A less charitable take would be that VC as an industry is driven in part by "FOMO," (fear of missing out), followed by rushes to the exits after someone yells "fire."

Herd dynamics in VC have consequences far beyond VC firms or the "limited partners" who provide their funds. Throw money too readily at a trendy industry, and you create a sudden abundance that distorts decisions by entrepreneurs. Pull it back in concert, and the sudden scarcity kills good businesses along with the bad. While VC funds only a minority of businesses, its preoccupations can resonate broadly.

One of the authors teaches MBA courses in innovation and entrepreneurship. Entrepreneurs approach him for advice on how to manage cycles of boom and bust, investor preoccupation with scale, and mania for the tech of the day. How, they ask, can they make capital raised in boom times last longer than they forecasted, when levels of investment in the industry or across early-stage ventures suddenly drop off? Or: why do investors turn up their noses at a business when they don't get a certain answer about using the tech trend of the day or reaching megascale?

Before 2020, crypto-focused VC funds raised less than $5 billion annually. This more than tripled in 2021, then multiplied over five times in 2022, only to drop back below its 2020 level in 2023 (Majic Predin, 2024). As a blockchain entrepreneur observed to one of the authors, during the hot years, you could barely turn capital away, if you were in the space. In 2024, AI-related deals effectively sustained venture investing, with a few large deals accounting for most investing (Grabow, 2024). AI drew 42% of US VC in 2024, up from 36% the previous year and 22% the year before that, according to a report from HSBC Innovation Banking (PYMNTS, 2024).

These trends have a huge effect on what gets innovated. In 2024 Pitchbook asserted that "AI startups account for 22% of *first-time* [italics ours] VC financing, reflecting a mass pivot among founders that is ringing alarm bells for investors concerned that the technology is increasingly being used as a marketing tool to raise capital" (Robbins, 2024). The rush to jump on board can starve innovation that fails to pursue a certain market, promise a certain level of returns, or follow a technology trend. Senior emerging tech analyst Brendan Burke worries that this mentality may be leading early-stage capital to pass on companies not using large language models. Such models support tools like ChatGPT. "Right now, there are too many startups seeking too few dollars and AI costs are plummeting, making it trivial for first-time founders to integrate LLMs into their products. Many non-AI companies can't raise a dollar today" (Robbins, 2024).

Early-stage VC is not necessarily diversified in the way a traditional investment portfolio would be. A core principle in finance is "diversification" – basically, avoid placing all your bets on what's similar enough to trend together. For example, a financial advisor may recommend that an investor diversify across multiple industries or geographies to reduce the risk that values fall in sync. Some analyses suggest there may be benefits to diversification for VCs, despite the emphasis on finding new tech trends (Pulcrano et al., 2024).

When companies in a portfolio are all hoping for similar technological breakthroughs, those companies are correlated, not diversified. The companies may move up or down together in ways VC risk models aren't adequately measuring. In 2024, BlackRock wrote down the value of its flagship Global Renewable Power (GRP) Fund III, acknowledging the reduced value of its investment. The bulk of BlackRock's GRP investments are in early-stage climate infrastructure (Brush, 2024). Blackrock's move reflected the poor performance of two companies in particular: New Zealand solar company SolarZero, and Sweden's electric vehicle (EV) battery maker Northvolt.

Figs. 4 and 5 summarize the deal dollar value and number of VC-backed companies based in the United States, by sector, from 2010 to 2023.[3] Within each column, the distinct patterns represent industry sectors. Diagonal lines, for example, represent information technology; light gray shading marks healthcare. Even as total VC funding shifts from year to year, info tech takes a relatively consistent share of the total dollars invested.

---

[3]Note: both sets of data are based on equity financings into US-based, VC-backed companies. Totals include investment by (among others) corporate investors, VC firms, individuals, and other private equity firms.

VC-Backed Deals, Dollar Value, 2010–2023
(Note: Adapted from EY Venture Capital Insights, 2024)

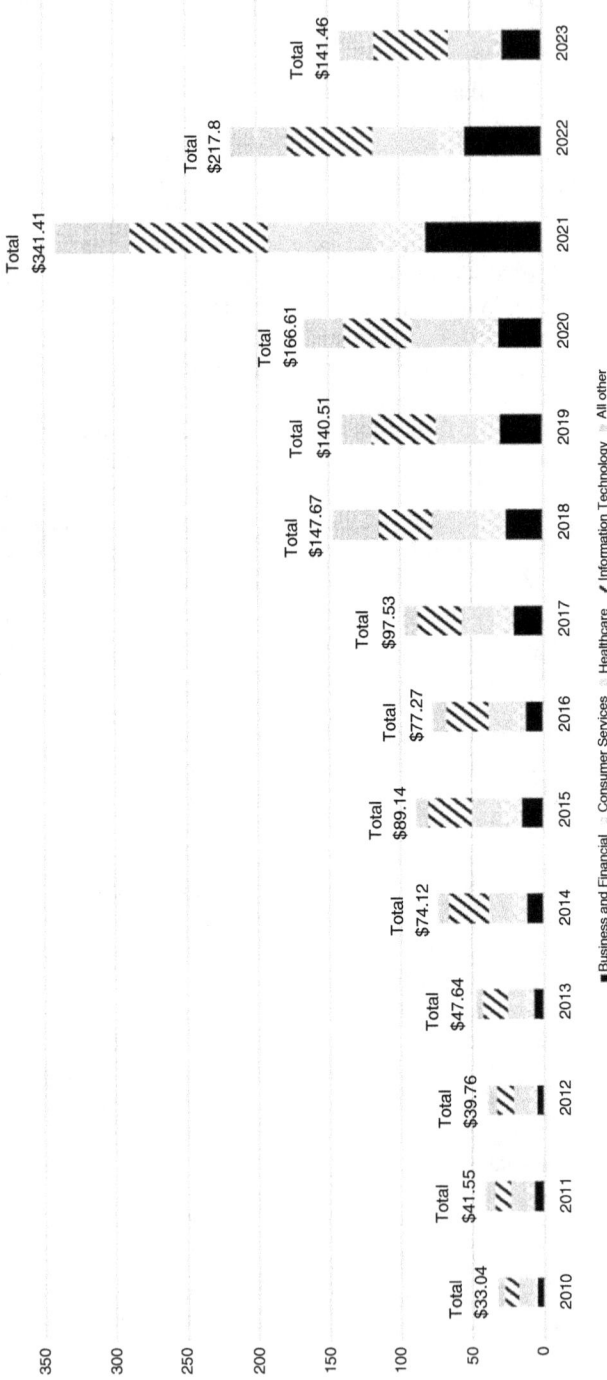

Fig. 4. Dollar Value, VC Deals by Sector, 2010–2023. *Source:* The authors, adapted from EY Venture Capital Insights, 2024 (Ernst & Young, 2024).

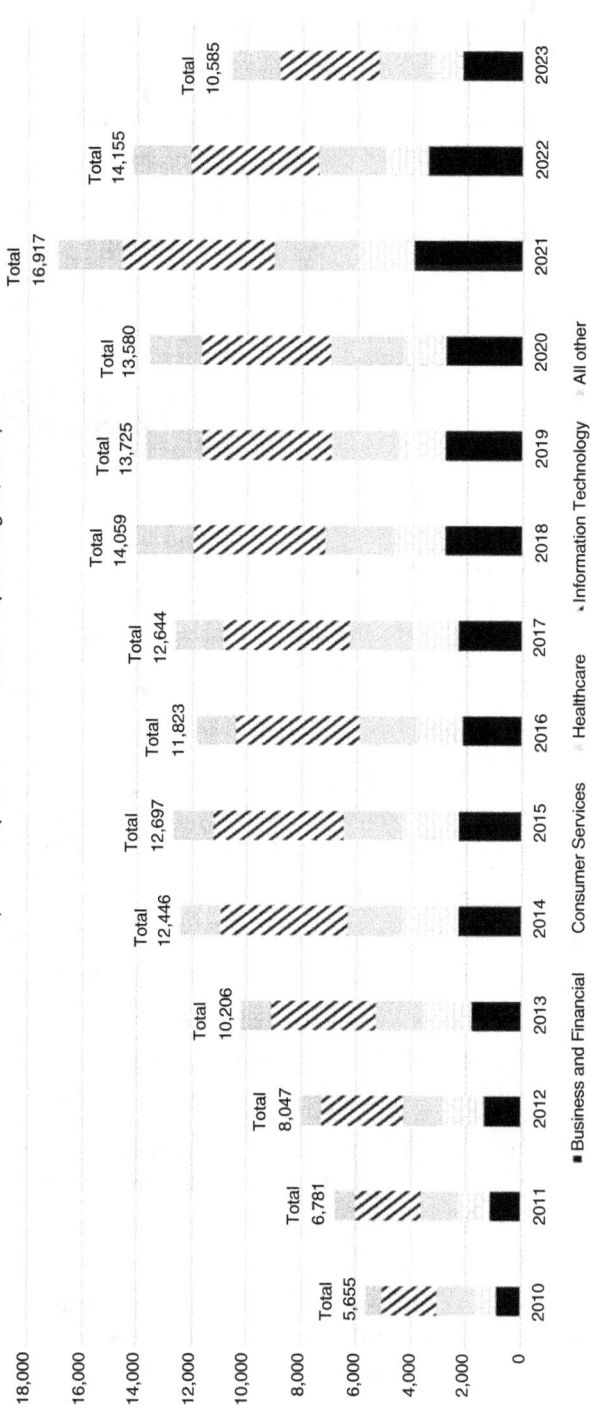

VC-Backed Number of Deals, 2010–2023
(Note: Adapted from EY Venture Capital Insights, 2024)

Fig. 5.   Number of VC Deals by Sector, 2010–2023. *Source:* The authors, adapted from EY Venture Capital Insights, 2024 (Ernst & Young, 2024).

The chart above focuses on the amount of money invested across sectors. The *number* of deals is similarly predictable by sector.

The VC model doesn't just affect what gets capital. It also narrows *who* gets capital. Let's start with geographic narrowness. Globally, "10 metros account for more than half of global venture investment,... 20 metros account for almost two-thirds, and ... 50 account for more than 90 percent.... Global venture investment is highly uneven and spiky, concentrated in a ... [few] leading cities and metros around the world" (Florida, 2016). In 2022, more than half of global VC went to firms based in North America, where just one in 20 people live. Asia, with more than 12 times the population of North America, got less than half the amount. Latin America garners less than 2% of the total. Africa, just over 1%. "The impact on employment is significant: start-ups (most backed by venture capital) represent about 1% of all European jobs today. Venture capital-backed companies account for 10% of all jobs in the United States" (Capolaghi, 2021).

Please Don't Go

Since more than half of VC investment goes to US firms, let's start there. Within the United States, venture flows are even *more* concentrated than they are elsewhere in the world (OECD, 2016). In the United States, "the top ten metros alone account for more than three-quarters (77.6 percent) of all venture capital investment; the top 20 account for more than 88 percent" (Florida, 2016). VC does not so much circulate as coagulate. It reaches about half of the country's 366 metro areas, heavily concentrated in the San Francisco Bay Area and across the Boston-New York-Washington Corridor. "Relatively large clusters of VC investment" serve "Los Angeles and Southern California, the Pacific Northwest, and Texas metros such as Austin, Dallas, and Houston" (Florida, 2016). Beyond the United States, venture funding clusters both by country and within high-investment countries (Capolaghi, 2021).

Because their model requires big wins, most VCs seek investments that can dominate local markets, and then replicate like Star Trek's Borg. A firm that gains investment uses the influx of capital to kill local competitors. If it succeeds, it moves on. As Shuman describes, "Winners, which become publicly traded, almost always desert the community where they originated. Then, the losers, the beneficiaries of years of local sweat equity, are squashed. Either way, communities lose" (Shuman, 2024). Venture for America (VFA) founder Andrew Yang describes his experience with this process. VFA would work with a local business until it became successful enough to attract VC funding. Then the VC would make funding conditional on the business moving to the Bay Area – taking the local jobs with it. Yang describes an example:

> There was [a] 100-person startup in Providence, Rhode Island.
> And then a venture capitalist in San Francisco offered them tens of
> millions of dollars with the partial condition that they move to San
> Francisco. So ... [t]hey moved.... And that company went from

100 employees in Providence to zero. And then the mayor of Providence was literally showing up at their office, being like, please don't go. Please don't go. But if you're that business, what are you going to do? (Douthat, 2019)

This process takes oxygen from innovators who can create *locally responsive* solutions. It's built into the emphasis on huge wins typical of VC as we know it. It's also threaded into how venture funding identifies *who* gets to develop experiments to shape the future.

They Missed the Best Players

VC concentrates capital on a few attempts at home runs, instead of seeding diverse potential innovations. In pursuit of such home runs, VCs invest and look for *brilliant* entrepreneurs. In this way, they operate much like old-school sports recruiters. Seeking players who *looked* the way great players should, scouts often overlooked the best ones by the numbers. The book (and later movie) *Moneyball* highlighted the talent this approach missed and the competitiveness it sacrificed (Lewis, 2004).

It's one thing when this affects who gets picked for sports teams. It's quite another when it determines what ventures and innovations see the light of day. As tech writer Ed Zitron quips, OpenAI's Sam Altman "is a college dropout with a failed startup, one where employees tried to get him fired twice. . . . Yet because he resembled the kind of guy that got things done, powerful people in Silicon Valley [and elsewhere] keep falling over themselves to give Altman the opportunities that made him look like a kingmaker" (Zitron, 2024c).

Such kingmaking creates a self-fulfilling prophecy. Altman went on to run the storied accelerator Y Combinator, which itself functions as a Silicon Valley gatekeeper. Then, in 2024, as CEO of OpenAI – at the time projected to lose between $4 and $5 billion that year – he raised $6.6 billion, the largest venture round in history. The raise included $500 million from Softbank, the VC that underwrote WeWork's growth (Isaac & Griffith, 2024).

Altman may succeed wildly in the end. What we'll never know is how many others might have realized a superior vision, much as we'll never know how the athletes passed over in Moneyball might have performed. What we do know is that when VCs throw money at a WeWork or an OpenAI, it is difficult for entrepreneurs everywhere to get funding for innovations that respond to pressing needs. If that sounds like an exaggeration, look where VC concentrates. Does innovative talent exist mostly there?

Hang on, though. Could investors possibly afford to miss innovative talent? They succeed by investing in business models that can get customers, make money, and transform systems. With that much pressure on the investor side, the entrepreneurs who get capital must be the ones that can do the most, based on tough objective criteria and analysis. Right?

Not so much.

It's Personal

Soft, squishy personal assessment drives how investors find the entrepreneurs they consider – and whether they choose to invest. This starts with the megatrends we've discussed in this chapter, and who has the "vision" to make the most of them. As Rick Heitzmann of FirstMark puts it: "We believe that the best opportunities don't always walk into our office. We identify and research megatrends and proactively reach out to those entrepreneurs who share a vision of where the world is going" (Gompers *et* al., 2021).

This focus on shared vision begs the question – how do venture capitalists find and select those who share their vision? Turns out, finding which founders to consider depends on introductions within a circle of familiarity. A 2021 Harvard Business Review survey of 900 people in the U.S. VC shows that most potential investments come from people with whom the investor associates – and the people they in turn know. "[M]ore than 30% of deals come from leads from VCs' former colleagues or work acquaintances. Other contacts also play a role: 20% of deals come from referrals by other investors, and 8% from referrals by existing portfolio companies. Only 10% result from cold email pitches by company management. But almost 30% are generated by VCs initiating contact with entrepreneurs" (Gompers et al., 2021).

OK, so getting in front of VCs depends on whom you know. But who gets funded? Could investors afford to make this a matter of familiarity, too? Investment due diligence analyst Peter d'Entremont puts it simply: "A narrow group seeds those who remind them of themselves, with the resources to build what comes next" (d'Entremont, 2023). Founders who've faced tough questions from investors might find this contention hard to swallow. Sure, you need to get into the room, but after that, how could funding possibly hinge on familiarity? Isn't it all about the size of the market, or whether you can defend your innovation against competitors, or the evidence that customers will pay for it? These questions matter, of course. The question is whether everyone bears a comparable burden of proof. Turns out you get a different kind of question when you fit the profile.

What leads others to remind us of ourselves? It's not just the schools they attended, the clubs they joined, or the activities they enjoy. It goes deeper, to what sociologists call "habitus" (Bourdieu & Passeron, 1990). Habitus is "embodied": we express it nonverbally, even in small ways, such as how we carry ourselves or dress. In essence, it's the embodied combination of beliefs, assumptions, behaviors, skills, and values we internalize and carry with us. Crucially, habitus is unconscious. We know what we like or value, but we don't know specifically why. When we enjoy going to the art museum, find power in certain types of music, or define freedom a certain way, that's habitus. It includes the cultural capital (Bourdieu & Passeron, 1990), social behaviors, and advantages that enable us to gain and maintain resources or opportunities.

Cultural capital involves a combination of noneconomic forces such as family background, social class, varying investments in and commitments to education, etc. (Bourdieu, 1986), all of which influence success. Acquiring cultural capital takes time, effort, and opportunity. When you see an individual with a skill, you encounter the outcome of that investment at the same time as you encounter the person. In this way, the person embodies the cultural capital. For example, if you're born into a well-connected, influential family, it's easier for you to talk to well-connected, influential people. This doesn't guarantee that you'll get ahead instead of someone else, but it makes it easier.

Investment decisions depend heavily on cultural capital. The board chair of the Corporate Finance Institute lays out what investors are looking for: "Most venture capital firms will say the decision largely comes down to people, as opinions on markets and technology are extremely challenging to get right, and are not necessarily that relevant. In terms of people, the two most important traits are . . . ."

Demonstrated acumen? Industry expertise? Previous results?

Nope.

The key traits, he says, are "courage" and "genius" (Vipond, 2014). Superstar investors like Andreessen Horowitz's Marc Andreessen stress this point. "There's . . . the surface level stuff . . . you look for a huge market and you look for differentiating technology." These Andreessen sees as matters of opinion. "The decision is and should be around people. The two things we really zero in on people are . . . courage and genius" (Stanford Graduate School of Business, 2014). Andreessen cites one of his partners, who defines courage, quoting Nietzsche, in terms of the "will to power." Does a VC as successful as Andreessen know it when he sees it? Or could they fall into the trap of kingmaking, of anointing winners and getting lucky sometimes, while convincing themselves that they recognized the Golden Child?

Mary Murphy, author of *Cultures of Growth,* studies the perception of genius. Her research suggests that genius is a story we tell ourselves, and then modify the facts to fit. We retell history to emphasize the one who, because of innate talent, has a brilliant "aha" moment that changes the world. We cling harder to this myth the more our daily lives require interdependence, collaboration, and teamwork (Murphy, 2024, p. 9).

All the Wrong Places

Genius narratives create self-fulfilling prophecies, Murphy notes, when those with resources give opportunities to the people they recognize, who then get to run with those opportunities. To return to the OpenAI example we introduced earlier, Ed Zitron frames its 2024 funding success as the logical extension of betting on what looks like genius. Open AI got the *chance* to do what it's doing based on the belief that "[Altman] has some unique insight, despite the fact that all signs point to him knowing about as much as they do, allowing him to prop up an unsustainable, unprofitable and directionless blob of a company as a means of getting billions of dollars of equity in the company . . ." (Zitron, 2024f).

Murphy's research sheds light on why a community led by already successful tech founders and investors might be tempted to operate this way. "Research I've conducted shows that the genius mentality helps maintain the status quo. Those who most benefit from the status quo – the few ... considered stars – have an interest, consciously or unconsciously, in keeping it in place. At the same time, it takes the pressure off those who haven't been anointed; after all, if I'm not someone who has it, people are likely to expect less of me" (Murphy, 2024, p. 10).

While this might take the pressure off, it's enormously risky for the world we end up with. As Silicon Valley lurches from bubble to bubble, how many of our most pressing problems does it solve? The genius myth doesn't just exacerbate the groupthink of recent tech bubbles. It leads investors to *miss* unfamiliar innovators and entrepreneurs – those likely more familiar with problems from which today's venture capitalists remain buffered. As life in cattle class expands and the poly-crisis worsens,[4] the innovations we most need may come not from geniuses with a Nietzschean will to power, but from people who know real problems in depth.

Silicon Valley changed the way we live. Tech transforms productivity and serves as an engine for macroeconomic growth. Yet as it moved from its upstart beginnings to one dominated by a few large firms, the dynamics have changed. VC's gatekeepers now limit our capacity to launch millions of small experiments, which often face a "valley of death" when it comes to capital availability. This may at least partially explain why *the same kinds of things keep getting funded.* We grow, Acemoglu observes, but in the wrong direction. "The direction of research and technologies that the tech industry has focused on, both because of ideological reasons and because of a particular business model that they developed, have pushed us toward technologies that I see as socially less desirable, in some cases actually undesirable. And as a result, we're actually getting growth without as many social benefits" (Zitron, 2024e).

In 2022, former Massachusetts Governor Charlie Baker co-authored the book *Results* with his chief of staff, Steve Kadish. In a discussion about the book with Rodger Duncan of *Forbes* magazine, Baker said: "Snap judgments – about people or ideas – are ... creat[ing] blind spots and missed opportunities.... Good ideas and interesting ways to accomplish goals in public life exist all over the place if you have the will, the curiosity, and the humility to find them" (Duncan, 2022).

Part III of this book focuses on how we can open up opportunities for people "all over the place" to turn their ideas into real-world experiments. To get there, we need to acknowledge our susceptibility to the genius myth, and the extent to which we've ceded the chance to experiment to those most insulated from life in cattle class. This goes deep. Well before the venture pitch, we signal to children whether opportunities to experiment are available for them.

---

[4]A polycrisis, according to historian Adam Tooze, occurs when seemingly separate crises seem to pile up for many people at once (Whiting, 2023). Edgar Morin and Anne Brigitte Kern coined the term, referring to "problems, antagonisms, crises, uncontrolled processes, and the general crisis of the planet" (Morin & Kern, 1999, p. 74).

Chapter 10

Break the Stranglehold on Innovation

The Makerspace and the Junk Corner

The state of Massachusetts contains some of the world's foremost innovation ecosystems. It also has the highest-rated public school system in the United States (FE News Editor, 2024; McCann, 2024). Yet as a teacher in Western Massachusetts tells it, cattle class dynamics are already at play by middle school.[1] The teacher describes her experience running a "makerspace." "The idea is you don't have a 3D printer at home . . . you don't have a laser cutter at home. . . . You don't have certain supplies or a computer to make your items . . . come and use it here. Saws, hammers, sewing supplies" (Massachusetts Middle School Teacher, 2025).

Materials are so limited she has to limit access to basic supplies. "You are not allowed to use the craft station unless you slow down and you stop and you fill out a form. . . . Because when kids were just like, oh, I could go to the craft station, do anything I wanted, stuff was disappearing so fast. . ." (Massachusetts Middle School Teacher, 2025).

The makerspace teacher contrasts this with the experience of a friend's child who attends an independent school in the Boston area.[2] The child told her about the "junk corner" at his school: a place where you can get glitter, glue, paint, sparkles, cardboard, items no one's using, and "just make anything you want to." The stark difference between the cattle class experience of her students and this child's premium experience broke her heart:

> I just looked at this child when he was telling me this and I had to leave. I . . . started crying because it made me so sad because I want every kid to have access to glitter and glue and sparkles so they could make anything they want instead of begging me for something shiny. (Massachusetts Middle School Teacher, 2025)

---

[1]Grades 6–8, generally 11- to 14-year-olds.
[2]In the United States, a school the family pays for, as opposed to one supported by the state.

One Size Fits None, 87–94
Copyright © 2025 Alejandro Juárez Crawford and Miriam Plavin-Masterman
Published under exclusive licence by Emerald Publishing Limited
doi:10.1108/978-1-83608-660-420251011

The contrast is so troubling because her job is to teach experimentation:

> I teach the engineering design process. Theoretically, it's okay to
> fail. Failures are beautiful ... but if you only get 10 pipe cleaners
> for your project, are you really gonna risk doing that?
> (Massachusetts Middle School Teacher, 2025)

Being resourceful with materials at hand can be powerful, she notes, but in this case, she finds herself saying "Be careful with the duct tape." The upshot is that her students don't get the chance to *practice,* and this has implications for their development. Judging by her three decades of teaching experience, she sees students making projects typical of a much earlier stage of development: "It looks like a second grader made that because you haven't had the years of using your hands and building and drawing and designing and having the resources available to you." This lack of freedom to practice stunts the development of skills and creativity. "If they're working with ... a finite resource then they are absolutely limited by their outcome because we know that practice makes perfect, right? ... We know that you have to do something over ... and over ... to have a final product that looks really good" (Massachusetts Middle School Teacher, 2025).

If this teacher's experience is any indication, young people learn quickly whether they'll get the chance to conduct experiments of their own. The sorting happens even earlier than we might think. While we can try to mitigate that sorting by adding people back into the pipeline, we've already missed many potential innovators.

Talk to the Same Folks, Fund the Same Stuff

Some do make it through their education and attempt something innovative. They often learn after a few pitches to internalize the notion that investors look for gigantic wins that bring hockey stick returns. The venture funnel demands such wins. In the 2014 talk we quoted earlier, investor Marc Andreessen explained that top VCs annually fund approximately 200 startups, out of about 4,000 in their funnel. Of the 200 startups investors fund, about 15 will make money for them. If the odds of being funded are 5%, and the odds of succeeding are 7.5%, the total odds of success via this model are approximately 0.04% (less than 1 in 2,000) (Stanford Graduate School of Business, 2014).

This funding math makes it more, not less likely, that venture capitalists (VCs) continue to seek so-called geniuses who can produce "unicorns."[3] Throwing resources at creating the next big thing stifles more diverse, innovative, and resilient ecosystems where a multiplicity of experiments can thrive. A model designed to launch a few giant wins demands industry domination through consolidation and blocking competition. It turns innovation into a kind of Hunger Games in which investors equip their portfolio firms to eliminate rivals.

---

[3]A unicorn is a startup valued at $1 billion or more while not yet listed on the stock market.

The hunt for the unicorn goes hand in hand with the practice we introduced in the last chapter, of betting on innovators who remind you of yourself. As a consequence, we invest nearly all our capital in those most insulated from crises the rest of us now face. Can innovators with little "skin in the game" build the solutions we need? "According to legend, for the Romans, engineers needed to spend some time under the bridge they built ... that should be required of financial engineers today. The English ... had the families of the engineers spend time with them under the bridge after it was built" (Taleb, 2013, p. 497).

Cognitive biases (including the affect and availability heuristics) make it hard for us to care much about predicaments we can't directly relate to.[4] And a demographic sliver does most of the investing. White men comprise 58% of the people who work in the US venture capital industry and control 93% of the venture capital dollars (Kerby, 2018). Further, 20% of people working in VC are Asian men, 11% are White women, 6% are Asian women, 2% are Black men, 1% are Black women, 1% are Latino men, and nearly 0% are Latina women (Edwards, 2021). Despite the demographics, early-stage investors make decisions according to rigorous processes of due diligence, in which everyone gets asked the same tough questions, right?

"I'll Ask the Questions"

Well, yes and no. Investors ask tough questions. Some entrepreneurs get more of those questions. To quantify this, Dana Kanze and her colleagues distinguished between "prevention" and "promotion" questions asked at TechCrunch. Prevention questions put entrepreneurs on the spot to defend their claims strenuously. Promotion questions set them up to advance their case. Turns out, women field a disproportionate share of prevention questions. In the TechCrunch study, two-thirds of the questions posed to male entrepreneurs were promotion-oriented, while two-thirds of those posed to female entrepreneurs were prevention-oriented (Kanze et al., 2017).

This difference in the kinds of questions entrepreneurs field affects the answers they give. Entrepreneurs who get more prevention questions start to justify themselves, trying to convince investors they won't lose money, while those who get more promotion questions focus on the upside. Most importantly, the questions gap correlates with outcomes. *Every additional prevention question asked of an entrepreneur cost the startup $3.8 million in funding, on average* (Kanze et al., 2017, p. 4). "Entrepreneurs who fielded mostly prevention questions went on to raise an average of $2.3 million in aggregate funds for their startups through 2017 – about seven times less than the $16.8 million raised on average by entrepreneurs who were asked mostly promotion questions" (Kanze et al., 2017, p. 3).

---

[4]The affect heuristic describes our tendency to make decisions based on emotion, not data (Hoffman, 2024). The availability heuristic refers to our tendency to relate to events to the extent that they seem memorable (Sohail, 2024).

In the broader market, less than one in 50 venture dollars goes to female founders. Still, could that be in part because male-founded teams make better investments? The numbers suggest the opposite. "Data collected by First Round Capital … found that the female-founder companies it had funded performed 63% better than the all-male founding teams it had funded," and "research from the Ewing Marion Kauffman Foundation has found that women-led teams generate a 35% higher return on investment than all-male teams" (Fatemi, 2019). Women effectively run an obstacle course in the race for capital, and it's not just innovative women who get written out of the script in advance. A mere 2.6% of venture capital goes to Black and Latinx founders overall (Crunchbase, 2020). According to digitalundivided's biennial Project Diane study, over the past decade, startups led by Latina women raised less than a third of a percent of VC funding, while Black women raised six ten-thousandths of a percent (digital-undivided, 2023).

Underfunding entire demographic groups continues despite ample research demonstrating that companies with more diversity prove more profitable (Hunt et al., 2023; Noland & Moran, 2016). Globally, company leadership teams are comprised of about 20% women and 15% ethnic minorities. The most diverse "executive teams [for women and minorities] are on average 9 percent more likely to outperform their peers" (Hunt et al., 2023, p. 13).

The Usual Suspects

The TechCrunch research suggests that narrowing the field of innovators requires no conscious favoritism. Every time an investor allocates capital only to those who make him feel comfortable, our economy underinvests in the most innovative among us. If you talk only to some types of potential innovators, you miss too many who could create needed solutions. Important insights typically come from those less steeped in shared assumptions (Poetz et al., 2014).

When top-down, one-size-fits-none models threaten our ability to remake broken systems everywhere, we need outsider perspectives as never before. Yet funding decisions remain in the hands of a few, and an insulated class of innovators primarily addresses needs its members understand. In the United States, 1% of the $70 trillion wealth management industry is controlled by women or minority fund managers (Edwards, 2021). This is especially troubling when two-thirds of that capital is projected to be female wealth in the coming years (Malito, 2017). Actual ownership and control of established firms – decision-making power – has barely budged from legacy male domination over the last two decades (Edwards, 2021). This suggests the scorecard is broken (Lerner et al., 2019) and that VC and PE as industries are not meritocracies.

Either VCs are not all that good at finding what they look for, or they've prioritized the familiar and called it brilliant. In an astounding instance of narrowness, venture capital is controlled by people who went to a few schools – and token diversity in the industry is nearly entirely drawn from graduates of those schools. 40% of United States' venture investors went to Stanford or

Harvard; over 50% of black investors in venture capital went to those same two schools (Kerby, 2018). Is it just elite school graduates who understand the problems the rest of us face?

Across the board, decision-making within homogenous groups falls prey to known pitfalls. Evan Apfelbaum, in an interview with Martha Mangelsdorf, describes flaws inherent in homogeneous groups, especially in making financial decisions. Apfelbaum's research found that "[r]acially homogeneous groups are less rigorous in their decision-making – and make more mistakes – than diverse ones..." (Mangelsdorf, 2017). Apfelbaum contrasts the respective decision-making processes to explain how homogeneous groups could come to the wrong conclusion. "Homogeneous groups [had more] inaccuracy ... and ...people in homogeneous groups were more likely to copy another person's mistake – presumably assuming that the mistake had some value that they just didn't understand .... [By contrast] [i]n diverse groups, people are more likely to not rely on those types of assumptions and [will] come to an independent assessment of what they think to be the case" (Mangelsdorf, 2017).

Apfelbaum continues, "In homogeneous groups, there seems to be this inflated sense of confidence ... but it's not because they are more likely to deliver better results.... Those groups may not be considering all the perspectives" (Mangelsdorf, 2017). Hollywood loves the story of the outsider breaking in and getting a seat at the table. But it's unclear whether our institutions for financing innovation will ever open up more than a few token chairs at the highest levels. In economies like the United States, women have long outpaced men in educational achievement, but still hold few seats on the boards and financing committees that decide where money goes.

What to do? To a point, a person needs to learn to navigate existing institutions and play by their rules to get ahead. Innovators can gain valuable access to decision-makers and resources by demonstrating a command of appropriate cultural capital, managing the requisite codes, and fielding cues with confidence. In some cases, innovators may even get away with taking greater risks if they master such codes. Theranos founder Elizabeth Holmes intentionally lowered her voice and dressed in black turtlenecks like Steve Jobs. She fit the bill for some of the world's most influential men. Accordingly, they didn't look too closely at whether her innovation worked or her business model made sense. One of the authors worked with a tech founder in her 20s who would say "I want to present like Elizabeth Holmes, but with a product that works." Ironically, Holmes' example shows how the command of cultural capital makes it possible to take risks.

The justice system finally punished Holmes for faking Theranos' diagnostic tests. But it failed to change the system that rewarded her "genius" with a lack of tough questions. For every Elizabeth Holmes, how many entrepreneurs get too few hard questions because they fit the type – and what is the cost in worthwhile experiments that never get made?

For traditionally excluded populations, gaining access to resources and opportunities often means learning the (unspoken) rules of the game and building crucial cultural capital. For those who do make it "in," maintaining access and moving up can require that they accommodate practices that reinforce those exclusions. For example, women in finance and consulting tell stories about being expected to join in drinks at strip clubs and other venues geared toward "bros," or miss out on work socializing.

It's one thing for an outsider to learn the rules, but if a narrow club controls resources for innovation, and that club only admits outsiders who know the rules, how will we challenge the rules? As long as capital remains tightly concentrated among certain demographics, there's a place for teaching entrepreneurs to pitch traditional VCs and angel investors.[5] It may be even more important to build new webs of experimentation and draw resources to them, in ways we present in Part III. If everyone focuses on trying to master the codes, it will be hard to disrupt the clubbiness and herd mentality that governs resources for innovators today. The 2004 film *Miracle,* about the United States 1980 Men's Olympic Ice Hockey Team, puts a fine point on this phenomenon. Goalie Jim Craig, wanting to keep his starting role, says to Coach Herb Brooks: "Fine, you want me to take your [psychology] test [which I earlier refused to take], I'll take your test, is that what you want?" But playing by the existing rules won't do the job. Coach Brooks responds: "No, I want to see that kid in the net who wouldn't take the test" (O'Connor, 2004).

In the Fig. 6, "success" for an innovator or entrepreneur means drawing resources to an experiment. If you look like a stereotypical entrepreneur, your risk-taking is seen as positive. If you don't, it's not. The extent to which you fit the familiar type affects the kinds of questions an entrepreneur must field, as Kanze et al.'s TechCrunch research shows.

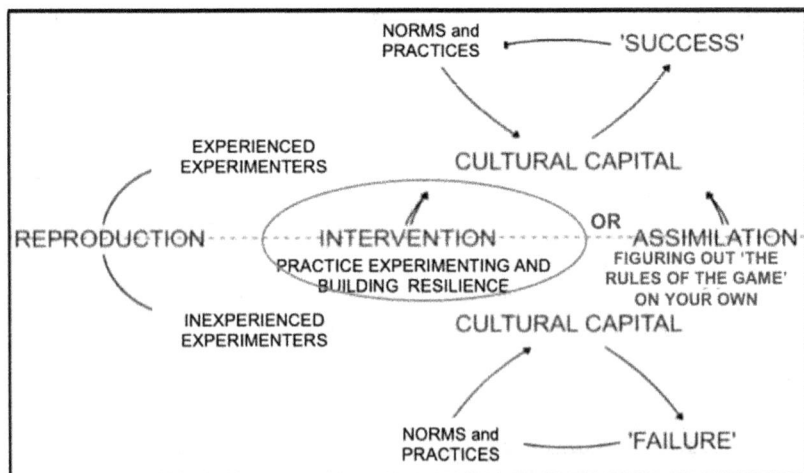

Fig. 6.   Paths to Cultural Capital for Success. *Source:* The authors.

---

[5]An angel investor invests their own money into an early-stage startup, hoping the idea becomes a reality.

The circle in the chart shows a second path – intervention – an alternative to assimilation. To innovate often means to change culture, not just acclimate to it. People can learn how to experiment, get more confident doing so, and change governing norms and practices. We describe how this intervention process works in Part III.

Not on Our Radar

Because of the clubbiness of VC, those diverse members likely to be admitted will tend to have a similar mindset as those already on the inside. At one level, it makes sense; a shared educational background or similar upbringing makes it more likely people already know the rules. However, the echo chambers within VC have pervasive effects throughout tech and the innovation ecosystem.

Early in Rent the Runway (RTR)'s history, Harvard Business School alums Jennifer Fleiss and Jennifer Hyman could not get investors to wrap their heads around their proposed business model.[6] "[V]enture capital firms often sent junior associates, receptionists, and assistants to take the meeting instead of … a full-time partner. 'It was clear they weren't taking us very seriously,' Fleiss said, recounting that on one occasion, a male investor called his wife and daughter on speaker to vet their thoughts" (Mascarenhas, 2020). As Hyman recounted, "male investors often based their assessments of the [fashion] industry on 'audiences of one', like their wives, since they don't use the product themselves" (Ghaffary, 2019) 2024 RTR annual revenues topped $300 million.

The RealReal founder and former CEO Julie Wainwright recounted a similar difficulty "finding VCs in a male-dominated industry who would put money into the company's Series A round, especially in the US. 'The luxury market is huge. You got all this data on it. And one of the VCs is like, 'You know, I just don't think the luxury market is that big'" (Ghaffary, 2019).[7] According to Wainwright, the VC was basing his analysis on a sample size of one – his wife, who preferred yoga pants to luxury clothes (Ghaffary, 2019). 2024 RealReal annual revenues topped $500 million.

Is it any surprise that "the amount of capital raised by minorities and women closely resembles their representation among VCs" (Kerby, 2018)? It shouldn't be. Multiple studies have documented a phenomenon called "stereotype threat." Essentially, when a person is told that others in their demographic category do worse in an activity, that expectation confirms itself. When they're told the opposite, social psychologist Claude Steele explains, the performance lag disappears (Vedantam, 2021).

The most ambitious, counterintuitively, are most susceptible to stereotype threat. Gupta and Bhawe have shown that this applies to entrepreneurs in particular: "Women with more proactive personalit[ies] were more significantly

---

[6]Rent the Runway is a subscription service for renting women's luxury clothing and accessories.

[7]The RealReal is an online luxury consignment site.

affected by exposure to the commonly known stereotype about entrepreneurs and had a significant decrease in entrepreneurial intentions compared to women with less proactive personalities" (Gupta & Bhawe, 2007).

"We Were Wrong"

Monocultures can seem stable – lawns look serene. They can also eliminate the pollinators needed for future thriving and adaptation. We know that biodiversity leads to more stable and robust systems.

Shuman, the economist, notes that early efforts to diversify funding focused on overcoming legal obstacles. "Many of us believed that legalizing investment crowdfunding in the United States would change people's investing habits. We were wrong" (Shuman, 2023). This proved to be necessary but not sufficient. "Creation of a local investment ecosystem requires significant education, marketing, and mobilization" (Shuman, 2023). Innovation lives in an ecosystem, and we should treat it as such. We know from ecology, agriculture, and other disciplines that monocultures pull nutrients out of the soil and weaken systems, making them less resilient.

Cultures of genius breed homogeneous thinking, and lack the "biodiversity" that enables robust and multiple ecosystem relationships to develop. Cultures of genius also seek the one great idea, the Google or Apple of climate change that will come and save us all. An approach that emphasizes biodiversity means that the more ideas you generate, the better your chances are of coming up with the solutions you need.

If we fail to rethink innovation, the risks are not chiefly for excluded innovators. They're for the rest of us who fail to enjoy solutions that might remake the way we live and work.

Part III

From the Direction You Least Expect

Solutions nearly always come from the direction you least expect,
which means there's no point trying to look in [the] direction [you
expect] because it won't be coming from there. – *The Salmon of
Doubt: Hitchhiking the Galaxy One Last Time* (Adams, 2002, p. 191)

Chapter 11

Equip People Close to Problems to Build Solutions

They Won't Build What We Need

Peer-to-peer energy "is one of the promising paradigms for future smart grids and refers to direct energy trading among peers" (Sahebi et al., 2023). On a peer-to-peer (or P2P) grid, "energy is traded on a small scale between residential areas, companies, factories,... consumers ... [and] customers who can produce their energy on a small scale and are equipped with small-scale renewable energy generation tools such as solar panels and wind turbines or micro-turbines" (Sahebi et al., 2023).

This model developed through experimentation where energy needs were pressing. "The first peer-to-peer grid was built in a village in Bangladesh, not in San Francisco, New York, or London," says SOLshare founder Sebastian Groh. This wasn't for lack of looking "in the direction you'd expect." Recounts Groh: "When I tried to do this with the resources and the people at Stanford, it didn't work. When I tried it in Berlin, it didn't work. It only worked," he says, "when we took it to the field, and had a local team, and we could iterate very quickly" (Wired Insider, 2024).

What we innovate hinges on where we look. Entrepreneurs often claim that their innovations will "disrupt" the way things work (by 2017, "disruptive" made an annual list of overused jargon (LSSU, 2016)). But "disruptive" means more than changing the game. It means changing who gets to play. The late Harvard Business School professor Clayton Christensen, who coined the term, insists:

> [Disruption] has a very specific definition, and that is it transforms a product that historically was so expensive and complicated that only a few people with a lot of money and a lot of skill had access to it. A disruptive innovation makes it so much more affordable and accessible, that a much larger population [has] access to it. (Christensen, 2012)

One Size Fits None, 97–106

Copyright © 2025 Alejandro Juárez Crawford and Miriam Plavin-Masterman

Published under exclusive licence by Emerald Publishing Limited

doi:10.1108/978-1-83608-660-420251012

To generate the disruption we need today means changing who gets to innovate. "If the people with the chance to invent don't face the necessities the rest of us face," Groh says, "they won't build what we need" (Crawford & Plavin-Masterman, 2024b). Is a world in which everyday people *do* get the chance to invent too hard to imagine? Would such a world represent too great a shift from the way things work today? Groh answers simply: "There's no choice. We have to.... The biggest challenge is how do we put the belief in all of us that we can do it?" (Crawford & Plavin-Masterman, 2024b).

As we'll show in the chapters that follow, our moment in history has both made this necessary and brought it within reach. To get there, we need to change the paradigm – especially for how we think about "scale."

Diseconomies of Scale

The question "but can it scale?," which we introduced in Part I, has become almost a cliche for investors to ask entrepreneurs. Economist Michael Shuman argues that when managers and entrepreneurs use a phrase like, "we've got to scale our business," "they mean to make it successful, it has to become bigger. But whenever you use scale as a verb, you probably are using it incorrectly because the theory of economies of scale is to find the right scale for the right mission, not the biggest scale" (Crawford & Plavin-Masterman, 2025d).

What scale is most *responsive* to the need it's designed to meet? Says Shuman, "There are things that improve economies of scale when you get bigger, and there are things that become diseconomies of scale when you get bigger" (Crawford & Plavin-Masterman, 2025d). A software platform that serves the needs of many can deliver powerful tools. At the same time, as more industries seek to automate the value they deliver, the pursuit of scale can lead us to settle for highly *un*economical outcomes.

Sure, your drug store wants to prevent theft, as shown in Fig. 7. And there are benefits to scale. It's convenient to have your prescription filled at any chain location with a click on your mobile app. But how many of us have forgotten what it was like to go into a drugstore where the proprietor knew you, thoughtfully advised you, maybe even cared what happened to you, and wasn't unduly worried that you were going to steal from the store, when there was a good chance she'd see you later and wave hello?

The systems of the drugstore and retail chains that keep essentials in locked cabinets are designed to serve as many people as possible with as few employees as possible. The employees involved don't have to know you or develop skills for dealing with you and your needs. They have to unlock the cabinet, wait while you pick the product you want, and maybe point you toward the self-checkout aisle. It's cheap – if you can get past the frustration. This model is designed to put local alternatives out of business, along with their capacity to know you and respond to your needs with more than automated recommendations. Take a model that relies on just a few people. Combine it with bargaining power over suppliers and the capacity to slash prices low enough and for long enough to outlast local

Fig. 7.   Toothpaste Locked in a Drugstore Cabinet. *Source:* Richard
D. Crawford, with permission.

competitors, and you make it prohibitively difficult for either longstanding neighborhood businesses or new local upstarts to compete.

Cattle class solutions come to seem normal and even necessary, but this is not the only way things can work. There's nothing natural about meeting specific local needs with large-scale models sourced from elsewhere. Shuman contends: "You can [produce] about 90 percent of what people actually consume in a competitive way within any given region of the planet" (Crawford & Plavin-Masterman, 2025d). He points out that on average, consumers spend 30% on goods and 70% on services, including not just your local grocery, but "financial services, health services, information services, personal services." When it comes to these services, responsiveness is everything. "Most of us want a service provider who we actually have a relationship with" (Crawford & Plavin-Masterman, 2025d).

Seeking software-like returns across sectors impacts people who work within these models and must function in limited roles alongside automation. And it impacts those who patronize businesses built on these models. On the consumer side, many of us have gotten used to the unresponsive systems we described in Part I. We don't try the helpline because it doesn't exist – or if it does, getting through requires jumping through too many hoops. A level of automation, where there's no person available to handle most situations, becomes normal. After a market becomes dominated by large-scale models, automating responses to customer needs can become an arms race. If you're in business, and the other guy is lowering costs this way, maybe you'd better, too. It would be easy to underestimate the pressure businesses face to keep costs on par with competitors.

The net effect is captured in the customer standing waiting at the locked cabinet – more life in cattle class. Our industries systematically chase large scale even when it is uneconomical. As Shuman argues, "in our era, the diseconomies of bigger scale are becoming more and more profound" (Crawford & Plavin-Masterman, 2025d).

The "Go Big or Go Home" Fallacy

The drive for efficiency creates powerful incentives for industry consolidation. Consolidation, in turn, creates more pressure to eke out efficiencies. That pressure increases incentives to serve large numbers of customers cheaply while finding new parts of their experience to charge for (on a recurring basis, if possible). When firms that dominate markets do invest in innovation, it's often toward driving more efficiency. Competitive pressures to respond nimbly to customer needs *decrease* with consolidation. We've seen this phenomenon with hospitals, doctors' practices, airlines, and even firefighting. These examples only scratch the surface. The large entities consolidation produces can get very good at innovating to reduce their costs (though if they have market power, they may be slow to pass those savings on to customers). Such entities can be far less effective when it comes to identifying problems that don't feed their models or solving problems in new ways that threaten their existing solutions. As Lina Khan, former chair of the US Federal Trade Commission, observes:

> Breakthrough innovations have historically come from disruptive outsiders, in part because huge behemoths rarely want to advance technologies that could displace or cannibalize their own businesses. Mired in red tape and bureaucratic inertia, those companies usually aren't set up to deliver the seismic efficiencies that hungry start-ups can generate. The recent history of artificial intelligence demonstrates this pattern. Google developed the groundbreaking Transformer architecture that underlies today's A.I. revolution in 2017, but the technology was largely underutilized until researchers left to join or to found new companies. It took these independent firms, not the tech giant, to realize the technology's transformative potential. (Khan, 2025)

When the paradigm is "grow large and dominate," firms tend to invest in AI by investing in"powerful chips and data centers," (Roose, 2025) which they think drive innovation. Why? Ed Zitron argues: "The mythology of both OpenAI and Anthropic is that large amounts of capital weren't just necessary, but the *only* (italics ours) way to do this" (Zitron, 2025). That's the Go Big or Go Home Fallacy in operation. Firms and the investors who fund them proceeded as if the only way to develop "powerful artificial intelligence was to hand billions of dollars to one of two companies, and [have them] build giant data centers to build even larger language models" (Zitron, 2025).

Seemingly infinite capital removes competitive pressures to be resourceful, so long as the illusion of stability lasts. The illusion crumbles when an array of small AI companies, including DeepSeek, remain scrappy, and adaptive, pushing for a breakthrough – like not needing such extensive computing power to achieve major AI improvements (Roose, 2025). Of course, it's not uncommon for large firms to benefit from the nimbleness of small ones by purchasing them. This can serve a useful purpose when it gives investors an incentive to take risks on upstarts – in hopes they get acquired by a bigger player. By the same token, it can narrow the game's goal, in some innovation ecosystems, to getting bought out by big tech. All the while our economy makes being small and responsive much harder than it needs to be, and not just in tech.

A Whole Chain of Productive Interactions

Trevor Vaughn's family has farmed in Texas for generations. He says: "The old model that has failed us, that has driven farmers to death ... is the 'go big or go home' model" (Crawford & Plavin-Masterman, 2024d). As agriculture attempts to mimic other industries' efficiencies, the pursuit of scale distorts economic relationships and dampens local resilience. Food becomes incredibly carbon-intensive to produce, package, ship, store, and deliver. The topsoil suffers, pollinators disappear, and water tables come under enormous pressure. Our long-term capacity to feed people degrades rapidly.

Producing food at an economical scale, by contrast, generates a whole chain of productive interactions. Agricultural Policy Solutions' Hunter Buffington works with local growers. In her experience, when you get the scale right, "you drive processing jobs because you've got local farms that are producing the food, then you need jobs to get that food to the local market, then you need the local market where it can actually be for sale" (Crawford & Plavin-Masterman, 2024d).

Left to find the scale that serves local needs, each enterprise drives demand for other related activities in the local ecosystem, spurring a virtuous cycle. Buffington says: "The beautiful thing is that if you're going to do regenerative agriculture, guess what you need. Manure, right? So then you have a relationship with your dairy farms, or perhaps your horse farms, that [meets] that need for manure, that creates another margin and offtake that is an economic driver" (Crawford & Plavin-Masterman, 2024e).

At first glance, the environment in which SOLshare's Groh operates could not be more different from that of Buffington. Groh's company serves electric rickshaw drivers in Dhaka, one of the densest urban environments on earth. Buffington works with farmers in sparsely populated US states such as Colorado.[1]

---

[1] 42% of Bangladeshis live in cities, and Bangladesh has about 30 times the population of Colorado, in roughly half the territory.

Yet both observe the local economy beginning to thrive when it produces goods and services in response to precise conditions on the ground, instead of adopting generic solutions from elsewhere. In *Cities and the Wealth of Nations,* Jane Jacobs argues that what she calls "city regions" thrive when they do just this – when they figure out locally responsive ways to meet needs, replacing solutions they used to have to import from elsewhere (Jacobs, 1985, p. 47). When people in a city buy locally generated solutions, farmers can sell their wares locally. Jacobs gives an example of a Toronto farmer's market: "In the market one finds . . . the diversity of rural goods a city buys from its own region, as compared with the sparse assortment of cash crops destined for markets other than a regional city or cities" (Jacobs, 1985, pp. 55–56). She applies the same insight to much of what is consumed in a city's surrounding region, from crafts to manufactured goods.

As producers in the city region create demand for solutions from other local producers, a kind of economic biodiversity develops that contrasts starkly with what communities get when they follow the go big or go home fallacy. During the COVID-19 pandemic, Shuman notes, "those communities that had more rigorously embraced the comparative advantage theory of economic development were the biggest losers because there are times where resilience and local self-reliance are really important" (Crawford & Plavin-Masterman, 2025d). Comparative advantage says that if you're good at one thing, trade it for everything else.[2] This raises the risk of developing monocultures of production – and losing the economic biodiversity that enables local regions to thrive.

Small Is Bountiful

The benefits of such biodiversity may sound like wishful thinking to minds schooled to seek flywheels and hockey sticks everywhere. How we *think* about scale determines what models we invest in, for everything from how we get the food on our tables to how we power our vehicles and homes. Too often, today's institutions operate as if economic monocultures enable people to thrive. We deploy everything from private capital to government economic development incentives as if a few brilliant innovators should create solutions for the rest of us. For some needs, a large scale is the right scale. But even when we recognize solutions that respond best to needs at a large scale, we should remember how often big started small (Crawford et al., 2024). If we forget, it's easy to fall into the intellectual trap of assuming that, though small may be beautiful, small can't meet large-scale needs. Not so.

A hodgepodge of independent drug stores, bookstores, or local banks is not necessarily less effective for serving large numbers of people than CVS, Amazon, or Citibank. Independents often lack comparable purchasing and pricing power. That can be conducive to the kind of interdependent thriving Buffington and

---

[2]In its simplest form, comparative advantage, applied to countries, suggests that each country should produce what it's best at, and trade it for everything else – even if it's also good at producing what it gets through trade.

Jacobs describe. Anyone who's ever been a fan of a local baker or tailor knows how a small provider can respond to specific local circumstances, develop distinctive practices, and spur cultural innovations. Lots of small solutions can thrive in and help grow biodiverse ecosystems while delivering large-scale responsiveness in aggregate.

While monocultures promise world-changing scalable solutions, there's often a catch. Large-scale solutions can be incredibly convenient when they work. When they don't, they often confront their users and employees with the question with which we started: What are you gonna do about it? The challenge, says Shuman, is to see this catch for what it is: "I say to communities, you really want to figure out what you're not doing that you should be doing in your community, [ask:] where are the leaks of dollars happening?" (Crawford & Plavin-Masterman, 2025d).

An organization focused on empire-building jealously guards its practices. In stark contrast, organizations with deep local roots often benefit from sharing best practices with organizations rooted elsewhere. Shuman explains that this "gives you insight about how to create new or expanded local businesses.... The difference between a failing local economy and a good local economy is that a good local economy learns from innovation all over the world and it becomes innovative itself from that learning" (Crawford & Plavin-Masterman, 2025d).

When local communities can retain that learning, instead of losing it to large, distant organizations, they can create thriving, responsive economies filled with rich and distinctive ways of meeting needs. They also, as the authors have argued, "build the skills and mindset to participate in further experiments. This shows how expanding the opportunity to innovate could create positive cascading effects to counter climate change's negative cascading effects.... Setting off such a snowball effect might well be the only way to quickly generate the millions of innovations now required to green ... economies and communities around the world" (Crawford et al., 2023). We must enable more people to access the financing, expertise, and experience to build solutions of their own and learn from each other as they do.

Creating locally responsive value doesn't necessarily make a great cover story for a magazine about genius entrepreneurs. Before he stepped down as CEO of Venture for America, Andrew Yang spoke of trying to do entrepreneurship outside a few major centers: "Entrepreneurship in these other cities ... [is] unsexy and gritty, measured in credit card debt rather than VC meetings, by getting customers instead of visitors or users, by changing the neighborhood instead of changing the world. Companies are started not with a desire to be huge, but because there's a problem to be solved" (Yang, 2016). Solving such problems is hard enough by itself. It's made much harder when we subsidize the already large. Those who produce local value in our economies do so in the face of staggering subsidies for economic monocultures.

Vast, Complex, and Deeply Entrenched

Take the vast, complex, and deeply entrenched global subsidies that keep the fossil economy on life support. Subsidies give industries that extract, market, and use fossil fuels the illusion of being economically productive while stacking the deck against those attempting to introduce alternatives. They distort markets to keep incumbent business models and products artificially competitive against would-be disruptive innovators. This practice artificially encumbers innovators endeavoring to reinvent the economy away from fossil fuels (Corporate Europe Observatory, 2023).

It's not hard to find organizations promoting their efforts to invest in alternatives – at least for audiences where that plays as good public relations (PR). The numbers tell a different story. Fossil subsidies, sweetheart financing, and slow-burn corporate change combine to create a steep uphill battle for innovators working to introduce alternatives. Lobbyists spend hundreds of millions of dollars influencing politicians in multiple countries to maintain unfair advantages for fossil fuel models. In the United States, legal actions combine with millions in campaign donations to governors (Pulliam & Mullins, 2017) and attorneys general (Weider, 2014). In parallel, leading banks double down on financing the fossil economy, according to Banking on Climate Chaos' reporting (Shraiman, 2024). Business proceeds as usual.

These strands form a Gordian knot. Instead of struggling to untie each strand, it's time to cut through them. Too often, big banks, governments, management consultants, and Fortune 500 companies offer meager solutions for our times. Instead of waiting for a big solution to come from them, it's time to open up the field to innovators who can respond to our needs. If we do, the solutions to our biggest problems could come in the form of numerous small, locally responsive experiments.

Open the Field

People are often willing to step up and innovate, even when no one opens doors. Dr. Andrews Ayiku, Lecturer and Small and Medium Enterprises Industry Coach at the University of Professional Studies, Accra, Ghana (UPSA), reflects: "You don't need much money to do this. You need a mindset, you need ... devotion, you need your effort. You need to be committed to solve this social issue" (Crawford & Plavin-Masterman, 2024a). It's not that money doesn't matter. It's that we need to spread that money out, to seed the widespread experimentation required. To be responsive, Dr. Ayiku emphasizes, requires engaging a broad base. "I let the community, the stakeholders, the opinion leaders own this. So it's easier for them to call for a meeting. It's easier to assemble them" (Crawford & Plavin-Masterman, 2024a).

This flips the usual paradigm. Local details constitute the fundamental data for building responsive systems. Solutions must fit local infrastructure, ecosystems, and practices because we need to innovate practices at every level in every industry and community. That's as true for innovating local food systems as it is for transforming our economies away from fossil fuels. It may sound too hard, or even impossible. One thing's for sure: if we don't try it because it seems too hard, it *will* be impossible.

What would it take to catalyze an era of broad-based experimentation, and awaken a world of people building local solutions, before it's too late? We'd need to start by changing *the way we think about who innovates.*

From a Distance

Why assume we'll innovate peer-to-peer solar at Stanford without extensive local knowledge and experimentation on the ground? Why turn to people in the same old places to reinvent practices everywhere? A kind of magical thinking pervades the way we approach innovation. *Antifragile* author Nassim Nicholas Taleb blames the "halo" we put around experts, which leads us to think they understand problems far from their expertise. Halo effects powerfully influence how we evaluate people (Nisbett & Wilson, 1977). We make "the mistake of thinking that ... a good chess player would be a good strategist in real life" (Taleb, 2013, pp. 271–272).

When "experts" swan in with fancy charts and analysis, we assume they know how to address needs beyond their specific expertise. When these experts come from global centers with leading institutions and resource concentrations, they may possess diminished capacity to relate to those needs. As human beings increase their power (and wealth), their feelings of compassion and empathy decrease (Foulk et al., 2018). Social scientists have run multiple experiments demonstrating this relationship. The more powerful people get, the less likely they are to need other people or their help. As a result, they have less empathy.

When it comes to climate change, people tend to want to do less about it as they get more powerful (Page et al., 2013). In disproportionately consuming countries like the United States, the powerful typically see their preferences reflected in environmental policies (Anderson, 2023; Paddison, 2021). Through the subsidies we have described, such policies have a dramatic impact on the playing field for innovators.

The inverse relationship between power and empathy could also create opportunities – if we can open the field to a wider group of innovators. Consider some of the reasons Groh struggled to make his innovation work at Stanford. "When we created the idea for SOLshare, we tried to develop the first product on Stanford's campus.... My professor there was of Indian origin and we were designing the product and ... [I said] we have the washing machine running, that will be nice for the energy usage pattern. And ... he was like: when was the last time you were in an Indian village? There is no washing machine. And, long story short, we didn't get it done" (Crawford & Plavin-Masterman, 2024b).

Solving the problem meant changing *who* shaped the solution. "The only time ... we managed to get the first prototype out, which actually worked, was when we had hired engineers who came from villages in Bangladesh who didn't have electricity, who really understood the problem" (Crawford & Plavin-Masterman, 2024b). For Groh, this highlights the need to equip people close to problems to launch experiments of their own. It's easy to assume that brilliant people at prestigious institutions have the answers, while the rest of us have at most a marginal role to play. It's the exact opposite.

Chapter 12

Everything Is Upside Down

Tuck School of Business professors Vijay Govindarajan and Chris Trimble famously coined the phrase "reverse innovation" (Govindarajan & Trimble, 2012). Their work upended theories that look to the most resource-rich environments for innovation. They pointed to the resourcefulness of people facing severe challenges and constraints, and the innovative power this brings out.

Why do we think of such innovation as "reverse" in the first place? In *The Open Society and its Enemies,* science theorist Karl Popper argues that at least since Plato, thinkers have favored big universal solutions (Popper, 1994). Popper argues that, as one of the authors summarized in an op-ed, "sweeping promises tempt in times of flux, but worthy advances come bit by bit, through broad-based trial and error" (Crawford, 2022). What Popper called "piecemeal" solutions entail trying out lots of experiments to see which ones work in particular situations.

The "Hail Mary Pass"

In a recent report, an international scientific team makes a Popper-like argument about solving climate change. To address the crises we face, the team of scientists argues, requires "radical incrementalism: achieving massive change through small, short-term steps." This contrasts with "the status quo, which isn't working" (Ripple & Wolf, 2024).

For top-down problem-solvers looking for the big solution, solar geoengineering has become a favorite panacea, garnering interest and resources from Bill Gates, the Alfred P. Sloan Foundation, the William and Flora Hewlett Foundation, and others (Gelles, 2024; Vetter, 2022). Solar geoengineering is an umbrella term for technologies designed to cool the planet by reducing incoming sunlight (Simon, 2024). Solar radiation management, a new technology, relies on spraying tiny particles into the atmosphere to reflect sunlight back into space (Nicholson, 2020).

Some scientists and backers have proposed deploying this in Africa as a testing ground, which gets a mixed response at best (Okereke, 2023). Even as excitement and investment increase, an international coalition of researchers and campaigners

One Size Fits None, 107–117
Copyright © 2025 Alejandro Juárez Crawford and Miriam Plavin-Masterman
Published under exclusive licence by Emerald Publishing Limited
doi:10.1108/978-1-83608-660-420251013

argues that we should not invest in or deploy such technologies. Geoengineering's proponents do not wholly understand the risks, have not articulated unintended consequences, and cannot prevent negative impacts, the coalition warns (Solar Geoengineering Non-Use Agreement, 2022). Solar geoengineering brings significant risks on the ground (Vetter, 2022). These could have major implications for places that may have little say in the matter (Okereke, 2023).

Centralized approaches can still make things worse, even when designed with the best of intentions – and even if they work as planned. Other systems may not interact with them as expected. Distinct regions may experience disparate effects, and those effects remain highly uncertain – on farming, accessibility of safe and clean water or food, and weather. Scientists also "object to intentionally releasing sulfur dioxide, a pollutant that . . . eventually moves [down] to ground level, where it can irritate the skin, eyes, nose, and throat and can cause respiratory problems" (Gelles, 2024).

However the side effects should play out, solar geoengineering is a medicine we'd need to keep taking. The technology requires constant deployment to limit warming because stopping would cause the bottled-up CO_2 to come pouring back into the atmosphere and make things worse. It also treats the symptoms, not the cause – sidestepping the challenge of reducing greenhouse gas emissions.

These concerns highlight a more fundamental one: Who determines how and where we deploy the technology? Who gets a seat at the table when decisions are made?

Paved With Best Intentions

Consider the unintended consequences of another top-down effort to address environmental damage. The global shipping community introduced new regulations to slash sulfur emissions in 2020. Known "as IMO 2020, [these regulations] cut the maximum level of sulfur in shipping fuels for all vessels, container ships, and cruise ships alike, from 3.5 percent to 0.5 percent with the goal of cleaning the air in ports and the communities around them, potentially saving hundreds of thousands of lives each year" (Valentine, 2024).

Three years later, cloud physicist Michael Diamond published research studying clouds along one southeast Atlantic shipping route. Diamond used pre- and postregulation satellite data to show that "even as it cleaned its emissions, the global shipping sector made marine clouds a little less bright. This change . . . means less sunlight is reflected into space – which means more [climate] warming" (Valentine, 2024). Other scientists have detected this phenomenon elsewhere since the International Maritime Organization adopted the rule.

Even with the best of intentions, centralized top-down innovations easily fall prey to conflicts of interest. Would-be savior companies, governments, and nongovernmental organizations (NGOs) often get their guidance from the large consultancies we described in Part II of this book. These consultants often help organizations account for impact by using versions of the same short-term yardsticks on investment, efficiency, and how to innovate. Relying on the same few organizations, often advised by the same advisory firms, interferes with the biodiversity we need to address the challenges we face today.

Just Let Us Run Your Company

Top-down thinking shows up not just in big, Hail-Mary-pass solutions, but also in how resource providers interact with innovators and their work. Business schools teach managers that they can generate superior results by applying their frameworks and tools to disparate situations. This affects finance, consulting, tech, and philanthropy, among other fields. Mary Murphy describes an interview she conducted that illustrates such top-down thinking well. Acumen founder Jacqueline Novogratz "shared a story of talking with hedge fund investors, about some of the challenges a supported company in rural Bihar, India was facing with rice husk gasification." The investors replied: "Well, why don't you just let us run your company?" (Murphy, 2024, p. 62). Novogratz continues: "They'd never even been to India, and had no experience with gasification. It was just the culture of genius writing you off," Novogratz said. "It was a deep assumption that even if they ... do what we ... do, they would be much better at it than we could ever possibly be" (Murphy, 2024, p. 62).

Do we see human achievement as led by a few brilliant people at the top? Do we look for solutions from "the best and the brightest" even when they're far removed from problems – in offices and corporate boardrooms far from factory floors; in air-conditioned vehicles out of sight of the wildfire's advance; in a metropolis that ships poorer places its toxic waste; or among tech founders who gush about AI freeing up our energies, even as they create a world in which many of our jobs get replaced?

Expanding on her example of far-off investors glossing over the specifics of gasification, Novogratz observes: "Their intellectual frameworks may work in their heads, but they don't necessarily work on the ground" (Murphy, 2024, p. 62). Engaging with facts on the ground through active experimentation can lead to questions and departures that don't fit the picture from afar.

The Acorn and the Oak

Most of us have seen someone come up with an effective or even brilliant way of doing things in a kitchen, a garden, a mechanic's shop, or an architect's studio. We encounter small, piecemeal solutions daily. Sometimes, those even become the way we do things tomorrow, but, as B. Lorraine Smith observes, we struggle to see that the grandest "oak trees" in our civilization evolved from acorns (Smith, 2023). Often, what became humanity's most valued creations *didn't fit the dominant paradigms of the time.*

What would an alternative set of priorities for investing in tech look like if, instead of replacing Altman's "median human," we enabled her to spend more time learning to *solve problems creatively, in new ways, based on locally specific circumstances and ideas?* When we think in these terms instead of following myths of genius, it's easier to invest in the myriad ways human beings can be resourceful when given the freedom to respond creatively to problems and situations. Murphy's research suggests that we do well to disabuse ourselves of the belief that a few geniuses should envision the future in which the rest of us will live and work. Cultures of genius tend to present themselves as hard-nosed and realistic. But it turns out the opposite is true: organizations dominated by fixed mindsets create self-fulfilling prophecies and *miss* the potential they don't see. "Cultures of growth embrace learn-it-alls over know-it-alls. Everyone, with the right supports, resources, and structures in place, has the potential to contribute to success" (Raikes, 2024).

If human flourishing *depends* upon unleashing creativity and that "richness of human capacity," could we use tech to foster that? Imagine if we focused investment on opening up avenues for people to use our minds in new and challenging ways – broadening the experiments we might conduct. The deepening polycrisis makes this not just appealing, but necessary. As Sir Ken Robinson observes: "I believe our only hope for the future is to adopt a new conception of human ecology, one in which we start to reconstitute our conception of the richness of human capacity" (Robinson, 2008). Only by equipping people to derive "piecemeal" adaptations and experimentation in every industry and locality, can we foster economic biodiversity and resilience in the present era.

Resilience From the Bottom-Up

Stable Doesn't Mean Resilient

Economic history is littered with well-intentioned attempts to *install* thriving ecosystems – to create the next Silicon Valley, revitalize a region, replace a dying industry, make a country rich, and create legions of jobs. But you can't force people to flourish from the top down.

Seemingly stable governments and large companies often promise that they'll make us thrive – but fail to respond to facts on the ground.

Taleb contrasts stable systems with *antifragile* systems that get stronger under stress. To keep the terminology simple, we'll call antifragile systems "resilient." Resilient systems don't just bounce back, they thrive in the face of change. Resilient systems *improve* under stress, the way bodies get stronger when we push our muscles and vary our routines.

Don't Put All Your Eggs in One Basket

Top-down solutions can provide the satisfaction of what's newer, bigger, more exotic, delivered faster, and available wherever, whenever.

Indeed, it's easy to assume that big, stable institutions – consolidated industries, mega-companies, and large government programs – make a stable economy. Shouldn't stable parts add up to a stable whole? Paradoxically, lots of *fragile*, experimental parts make the whole system resilient under stress. They provide flexible responsiveness precisely because they effectively try out many responses to changing needs, rather than following a preset recipe.

Small experiments aren't only about resilience in the face of stress: thriving goes beyond surviving. Without small experiments, you don't get bebop or breakdancing, lightbulbs or microphones, subways, or Scrabble (to cite examples from the authors' hometown). You don't get Catskills humor, New York pizza, or any of the brilliant inventions that light up with local specificity before they take on the world.

If you're not trying lots of things, you miss the kind of value that's hard to see in advance. As Taleb explains: "The fragility of every startup is necessary for the *economy* to be antifragile, and that's what makes, among other things, entrepreneurship work: the fragility of *individual* entrepreneurs and their necessarily high failure rate" (Taleb, 2013, p. 94, italics ours). This idea flies in the face of the notion that we can thrive by being successful as often as possible. Resilience proceeds from lots of attempts, many uncertain of success. For this reason, individuals need to be in a position to take intentional risks. Taleb dreams of holding an Entrepreneur's Day, with the following message: "Most of you will fail ... but we are grateful for the risks you are taking and the sacrifices you are making for the sake of the economic growth of the planet and pulling others out of poverty. You are at the source of our antifragility" (Taleb, 2013, p. 113).

What enables more people to take such risks? New research we'll present in the final chapters of this book suggests an answer. Crucial inputs include opportunities to practice, chances to fail and learn, and places to turn for help. As people conduct experiments, an innovation ecosystem begins to develop around their interactions. Whether the innovation happens locally or through a dispersed community like an alumni group, it grows across many interactions.

If we want to generate resilience, we need to notice what enables people to thrive, not according to some oft-told story, but in the real world. Economic developers, Michael Shuman notes, say that wealth blooms when big global companies come to town (Crawford & Plavin-Masterman, 2025d). Ask the wrong question, get the wrong answer. The question we should be asking is how to enable everyday people to generate too many experiments to count. Throw a stone and measure the circle it makes when it sinks into the water. Direct, but it doesn't account for ripple effects. Spend all your time picking the biggest stone, you risk watching it sink to the bottom.

Biodiverse systems thrive by being locally responsive: they adapt to fit specific interactions and needs. Few question this when it comes to the natural world, but it applies to human society, too. Think of a diver practicing dives. If you can't practice difficult dives, you'll never master them. If you can't splash into the water when you try something new, you'll never invent your own. A performance skill that involves experimentation depends upon the chance to take risks and bounce back. It becomes rational to take those risks when you can interact with a community that works to guide and equip you, supports your efforts, and offers the chance to fail and try again. As you practice your dives, you learn to try difficult and original ones. As the authors have argued, "When people close to serious problems get opportunities to participate in experiments to solve them, they develop the mindset, skills, and thirst for more experimentation" (Crawford et al., 2023).

Fig. 8 illustrates what can happen when a broad base of people gets the chance to try and fail, work with others who can help them, regroup, and try again. We call this the double funnel model because it's not just what comes out of the narrow spout that counts. It's what gets magnified from there – and cultivated along the way. More experiments build more resilience, and more resilience enables more experiments to thrive.

In this book, we've critiqued the overreliance on "flywheel" business models that become less responsive the faster they spin. Could we instead create a flywheel for generating more experiments, where each experiment responds to emerging needs?

I Built This … With Help (Oh, What a Nightmare)

In the film *My Cousin Vinny,* Joe Pesci plays a newbie attorney who wins a case against all odds. At the end of the film, as he drives off into the sunset with his fiancée, Marisa Tomei's character, he's in a snit. "What's your problem?" Tomei's character asks. Pesci responds: "My problem is I wanted to win my first case, without any help from anybody." Tomei shoots back:

> This could be a sign of things to come. You win all your cases but with somebody else's help.... Oh my God, what a f****** nightmare! (Lynn, 1992)

For many of us, asking for help is such a nightmare that we avoid it. In an interview during the period after he got fired from Apple, Steve Jobs observed: "Most people never pick up the phone and call, most people never ask …" (Santa Clara Valley Historical Society, 1994b).

Why? Jobs emphasizes relative readiness to go out on a limb, what we've called the experimental mindset: "You gotta be willing to fail, you gotta be willing to crash and burn, with people on the phone, with starting a company, whatever. If you're afraid of failing, you won't get very far" (Santa Clara Valley Historical Society, 1994b). Investor Marc Andreessen, in the talk we quoted earlier, adamantly disagrees. He's all about courage as Nietzschean will to power, not the kind that flirts with failure. Andreessen insists, "There's always been this … thing in Silicon Valley … failure is a wonderful thing … failure teaches you all this stuff … it's great to fail a lot.... We don't, like, buy any of that, we think that's all complete, complete nonsense. We think failure sucks" (Stanford Graduate School of Business, 2014).

Which is it? According to Scott Anthony, professor at the Tuck School of Business, it's not enough to aim for opportunities. They have to hit near us. The key is to clear an area large enough that when opportunities fall from the sky, as eventually they will, they land on it. Anthony cites the example of Julia Childs,

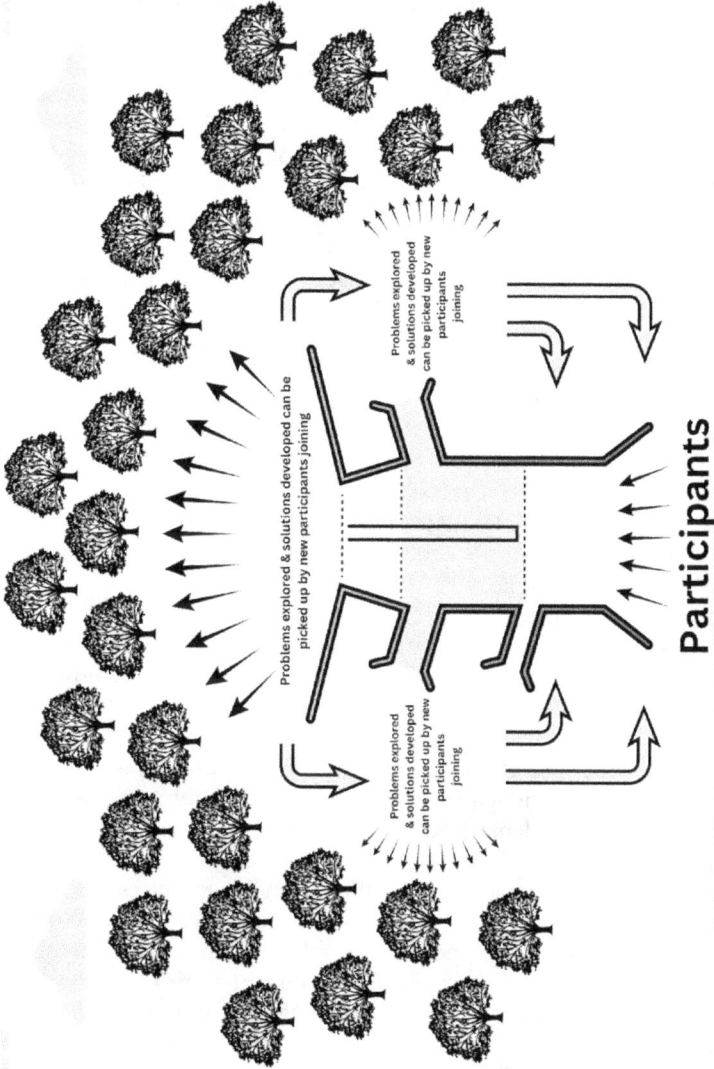

Participants

Fig. 8. Double Funnel. *Source:* Image developed by Tomás Mora Selva and reprinted with permission from the Democratizing Innovation Institute.

the chef, TV personality, and writer: "Fortune smiled on Julia many times, but Fortune smiled because Julia followed the behaviors common to great innovators. She was intensely curious. She collaborated. She was a disciplined experimenter. She created the surface area for serendipity to strike" (Anthony, 2024).

Let's call this "serendipity surface area" for short, and return to Steve Jobs, age 12. The future Apple founder describes an experience he had growing up in Palo Alto in the 1970s. To get spare parts for his computer, Jobs looked up Hewlett-Packard (HP) cofounder Bill Hewlett's number in the phone book. He dialed the number – and got the parts, along with an opportunity to get some experience at HP (Santa Clara Valley Historical Society, 1994).

If you didn't grow up in a time and place where you could call the founder of HP and reach him, widening your serendipity surface area is harder, but even more vital. The entrepreneurship professor in Ghana we quoted earlier, Andy Ayiku, makes his students figure out whom they need to talk to, he says, and "go and talk to them" (Crawford & Plavin-Masterman, 2024a). This expands the serendipity surface area: "Surprisingly, when they are able to do this from the beginning, they are able to get free land, free accommodation, especially when the [community leaders] understand what you are coming to do."

When we pull off the impossible, all we can think of is what *we* had to go through to beat the odds. Indeed, innovation entails resourcefulness – combined with enough surface area for serendipity to strike. The 12-year-old needs to call the HP founder to ask for spare parts *and* that founder needs to be listed in the phone book. It can be tempting to focus on just part of this. We end up emphasizing either initiative or help – either "I built this" or "It takes a village." Yet most of the time, *both* are needed. Oh, what a nightmare.

The stories we tell ourselves about people striving against great odds have this idea built in. In our most enduring stories and myths, as Joseph Campbell and others have argued, the unlikely hero faces seemingly insurmountable obstacles. Just when things become impossible, help comes from the hands of a stranger the hero meets along the way. There are two essential ingredients here. One is the individual's initiative: 12-year-old Jobs made the call. The other is access to an ecosystem with resources – enough surface area for serendipity to strike. Turns out, resourcefulness and interdependence are two sides of one coin. Creating new solutions requires both.

Resourcefulness entails overcoming difficulties by finding resources where they seem to be missing: putting an object to an inventive use, securing help from a surprising source, discovering unexpected strengths, finding opportunity in a challenging predicament, or coming up with a solution that doesn't need the usual resources to execute. Readers with business training will have done "SWOT" analyses, enumerating strengths, weaknesses, opportunities, and threats, each in their respective boxes. Resourcefulness entails finding and using what's not in the boxes. Of course, innovators do face well-resourced competitors, and require financial resources for everything from developing prototypes to getting on users' radar. Still, the young Jobs gets the spare parts where others didn't think to look, by asking the question others didn't think to ask. Then resourcefulness opens up unexpected avenues like Hewlett offering him part-time work on the HP assembly line.

Where does the innovator turn, when they can't look up the cofounder of HP in the phone book, and when leading gatekeepers have come to believe, along with Andreessen, that "failure sucks?" Today's Palo Alto today may be a far cry from the open playground for tinkerers Jobs recalls. But playgrounds develop when people play. Innovation ecosystems crop up when resourceful people help and depend on each other. Richard Florida describes the importance of "clusters" of creativity, driven by "people in science and engineering, architecture and design, education, arts, music and entertainment whose economic function is to create new ideas, new technology, and new creative content," surrounded by a broader group of "creative professionals" working in business, finance, and law (Florida, 2003, p. 7).

Picture these clusters within a web or latticework of connections. You can see the dots in a stylized social network diagram shown in Fig. 9:

To what extent has the digital age opened up the opportunity to form *clusters* across geographies? For centuries, to get access to a cluster, you had to make your way to a metropolis. Think of books and films about a young person trying to break in, and the first, chance connections she makes. Quite recently, the way we connect has become hybrid, combining digital and physical interaction. Can innovation ecosystems become hybrid, too? Can clusters like the ones Florida describes develop beyond the geographic spaces he studied?

Evelina Van Mensel researches "social" innovation and coaches aspiring innovators. The entrepreneur Martin Nedev was her student at American University in Bulgaria. They talk about building the innovation ecosystem in Sofia, where both are based. They also refer to a *global* ecosystem. As Van Mensel says, "There are so many interactions across geographies and when we talk access to mentorship, well, this can be an access to mentorship from across the world now … Martin … doesn't have only me now, but he has all the rest of this global team that he can go to" (Crawford & Plavin-Masterman, 2025a). This access to a wider network is useful, but it's the active collaboration that turns it into an innovation ecosystem. As Audia and Rider point out, "the process of creating a new company is inherently social" (Audia & Rider, 2005, p. 7).

Could a digital ecosystem enable people to get the resources and opportunities they need, without moving to Berlin or New York, Shanghai, or Silicon Valley? Earlier, we quoted Andrew Yang's account of venture capitalists offering to invest *if* the entrepreneur moves the venture (and the jobs it creates) to Silicon Valley. Laudie Jamous, UK Chapter Lead for Women in Renewable Energy (WiRE) speaks of a kind of innovator's brain drain. Young people around the world, if they aspire to create experiments of their own, must move to global centers to find resources (Jamous, 2024). When experimentation webs become tightly knit in a few places, but are missing elsewhere, we narrow innovation and discoveries.

In all the ways we have described in this book, the all-out pursuit of large-scale efficiency through automation inhibits new webs from forming. Our opportunity lies in the in-between places, where no webs connect. When we link webs of mutual support for experiments beyond the same old clusters, we build resilience. This can be even more vital for locales facing poverty, repression, displacement, and war. Dalia Najjar works with social entrepreneurs in the West Bank, Belarus, and

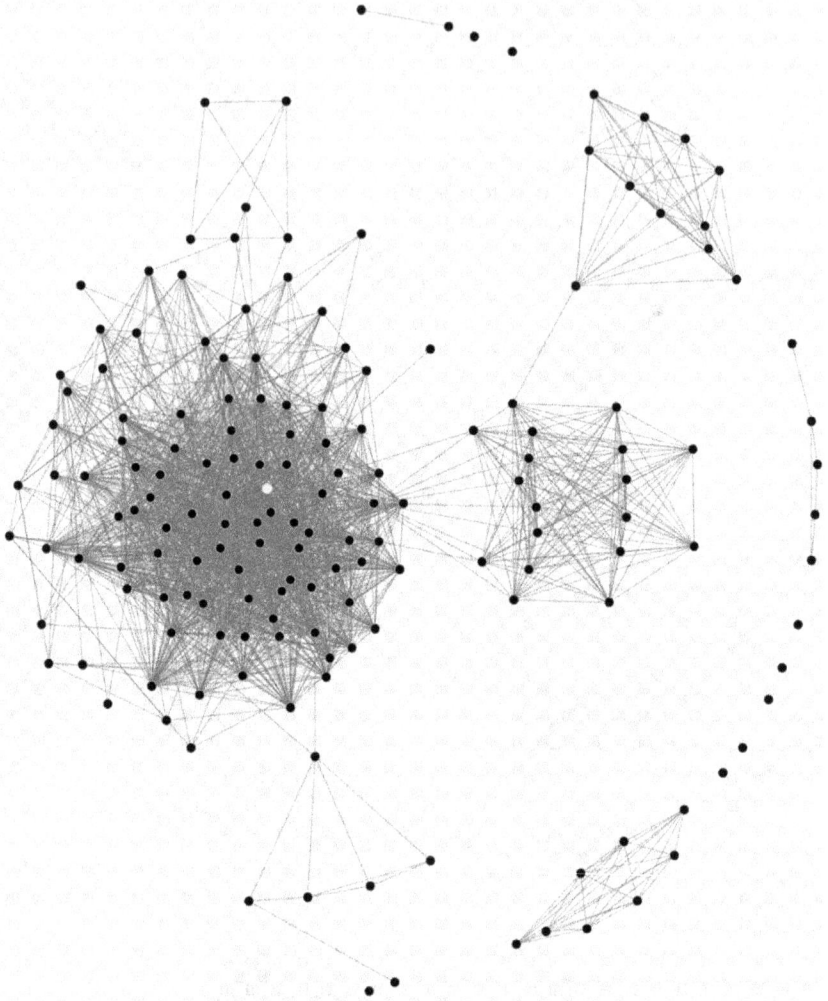

Fig. 9.   Social Network Diagram. *Source:* DarwinPeacock, Maklaan,
CC BY 3.0, https://commons.wikimedia.org/w/index.php?curid=37438799

Kabul, and has continued to do so through the wars in Palestine and Ukraine. She doesn't shy away from the bravery or the sensitivity these problem-solvers need to muster: "You need to be really brave to go through this journey . . . and meet with those people who are suffering and look at their needs and make sure that you are actually filling the needs of those people that you are serving" (Crawford & Plavin-Masterman, 2024c). She stresses that the work of imagining and building a different world persists in the face of what might look like impossible conditions:

"It does not matter where you come from or what struggles you are facing or what you are suffering from. You … need the will to make change. Each of us is from different parts of the world, but we all gather around the same will or around the same result that we want to see" (Crawford & Plavin-Masterman, 2024c).

If it's worth working to expand the serendipity surface area in the places Najjar's students make their attempts, it's worth striving to do so everywhere. As Groh says, we don't have much choice. To address "the necessities the rest of us face" we need to broaden who gets the chance to experiment. *The chance to experiment builds the experimental mindset, which leads to more experiments.*

Chapter 13

The Kitty Hawk Principle

We Have the Technology

Internet idealism can feel like a thing of the past. Excitement about the digital age's promise to democratize learning, creativity, or access to opportunity can seem almost quaint today. Public and private organizations now use our connectedness to track our behavior, mine our data, and train their platforms on our content. Multiple studies have shown that having a digital connection within reach *diminishes* logical thinking, concentration, and problem-solving skills (Carr, 2021). Regular smartphone use, in particular, has been shown to interfere with concentration; limit free play and independent exploration; diminish clarity of purpose, deepen divisiveness, and wreck mental health (Haidt, 2024). So much for the idea of digital connections enabling us to confront top-down systems and engage in decentralized collaboration.

Has digital connectivity failed us? Or have we allowed that connectivity to get hijacked for purposes other than our own? Even a printing press can function to cultivate critical thinking or spread hate. Most people in the world now have access to a digital connection. Does how we use those connections remain open for determination? Tech can enable a few Goliaths to block and intimidate upstarts. It can make it hard for would-be Davids to find their footing. Tech also presents the opportunity to open the field to more Davids and give them practice moving through it. To do so would unleash great power, as the experiments we present in this chapter illustrate. In previous industrial revolutions, a communications advance – the printing press, the telegram, the radio – opened up possibilities for unprecedented economic mobility, but the technology didn't do so *by itself*. People needed to use it in ways that expanded access to what had previously been reserved for the few.

Today, internet access reaches well beyond privileged enclaves, but our limited vision of who can innovate stands in the way of its democratizing potential. This barrier is surmountable. When we enable people to practice the experimental mindset, it unleashes extraordinary power. Research led by Crawford's company, RebelBase, demonstrates this.

One Size Fits None, 119–133

Copyright © 2025 Alejandro Juárez Crawford and Miriam Plavin-Masterman
Published under exclusive licence by Emerald Publishing Limited
doi:10.1108/978-1-83608-660-420251014

A team led by Tuba Erbil, Thomas Gold, and Tuba Senbabaoglu conducted this research from 2020-2023, with generous support from The Open Society University Network (OSUN) and The Bard MBA in Sustainability. Participant surveys and analyses were conducted using a competency framework developed by Crawford in collaboration with this team. Participants connected to a shared innovation ecosystem incorporating participating institutions around the world. They joined from a variety of sites – business programs in dense metropolises,universities in regions under siege, and internet cafes in remote townships. What began as a certificate program serving OSUN member schools grew to incorporate a wider group of organizations. These formed the Democratizing Innovation Institute in 2024 to build on their work together.[1]

To protect participant identity and to support data validity, survey responses were strictly anonymous. Here's what four years of responses from participants showed: Across cultures and educational levels, people develop the experimental mindset by attempting to derive real-world solutions to problems they identify – and by working with others who think differently and bring new skills and experiences.

In a series of op-eds co-written with cleantech investor and *Climate and Capital Media* Executive Editor Barclay Palmer, the authors identify an important principle at work. "We call this the 'Kitty Hawk Principle,' after the place where a couple of bicycle mechanics beat out well-funded competitors to make people fly. In the hills and fields near Kitty Hawk [North Carolina], they conducted thousands of tests with planes of their own design, that look more or less like bicycles with homemade wings" (Crawford et al., 2023).

We can use digital connectivity to open up a modern version of Kitty Hawk, and by doing so, initiate a seismic shift. The economy as we know it serves diverse needs with large-scale, highly "efficient" solutions, and turns to "geniuses" from the same old places to guide us. How well is that working for us?

Answer a request for proposal (RFP), make a funding submission, or pitch tech investors today, and you will quickly run up against the need to master an established set of codes. Even opportunities custom-built for the "underrepresented" attract applicants who learn the script. If there's an opposite of Kitty Hawk, this is it. It's the precise reverse of how we should decide who gets resources. We need people who can remake the way we do things today. Entrepreneurial people, UVA professor Saras Sarasvathy's research shows, distinguish themselves from those working to achieve established goals, because they *figure out* their goals as they proceed experimentally (Sarasvathy, 2008). We develop the experimental mindset by taking part in experiments. What if, instead of telling people what to do, we asked them what they envisioned, and gave them the tools to figure out what works, find collaborators, make the case for their experiments, and try them out?

---

[1]http://www.democratizinginnovation.org

A Digital Airfield

The world has become far more complex since the Wright brothers developed flight through trial and error on the fields near Kitty Hawk. Still, Crawford and company's experiments suggest we may be glossing over what's worked before. Those experiments indicate that Kitty Hawk remains highly relevant today.

It's commonplace for programs in entrepreneurship, innovation, leadership, and change management to cultivate new experiments via project-based courses, incubators, and accelerators.[2] Programs typically feature project deliverables (often team-based), coaches and mentors, and competitive presentation forums. A single institution or organization – a university, or a community youth program run by a nongovernmental organization (NGO) – typically sponsors such programs. Umbrella institutions exist to connect various programs. Examples include competitive forums (the United States' Cleantech Open), "apprenticeship" programs (Europe's Erasmus for Young Entrepreneurs [EYE]), and youth programs (the AFS Youth Assembly). Notwithstanding such umbrella programs, most people who could potentially launch their own experiments lack a common, systematic framework that connects them across ecosystems and geographies.

Since 2020, a community of practice facilitated by Crawford has deployed a new model across 20+ countries.[3] This model tests what happens when we link organizations and their ecosystems using a common platform for building experiments to change the way things work.

This work is ongoing. In the following paragraphs, we'll refer to the portion of it that occurred from 2020–2023, the period of study we analyze in this book. During this period, facilitators at participating institutions brought experience running experiential learning programs within their respective universities, companies, and business communities. Together they worked to see what would happen if they connected the people they served through a flexible shared system of tools, content, networks, and resources. They tested the hypothesis that they could awaken the experimental mindset and expand the serendipity surface area among participants.

The goal was simple: engage participating universities, chambers of commerce, community organizations, and employers with a common process for people to create their own experiments. Throughout this process, offer meaningful opportunities for participants to interact as they refine their experiments. Give participants shared tools and structured rounds of feedback, and measure the impact on those who participate.

Facilitators at participating institutions designed this process to prototype and test an idea: If they could offer an intersecting ecosystem across institutions and regions, it could open up "Kitty Hawk" opportunities and foster the experimental

---

[2]Project-based courses assign students practical projects ranging from developing a startup or business plan to working with an existing organization to effect change or help it grow. Accelerators and incubators help startups grow and develop. Incubators typically support early-stage startups, while accelerators serve startups that are already established.
[3]A group of people who share a common interest or goal and work together to improve skills and knowledge.

mindset. Through the demonstration project that followed, they worked to answer three linked questions.

(1) Could they meaningfully connect people across disparate organizations and regions, through a common process for identifying problems and developing experiments to solve them?
(2) If they could connect people in this way, would it help experimenters draw talent, opportunities, and resources necessary to test their ideas, and develop the ones that showed promise?
(3) Could such a process enable many people to take part in creating experimental solutions, when they otherwise would not have, and would the experience of creating them foster the experimental mindset?

To explore these questions, the community tested and modified a set of shared tools and content using an experimental, proprietary innovation platform called RebelBase. Facilitators used the platform in three ways: first, to offer content, tools, and collaboration workflows custom-designed for the purpose; second, as a digital forum where participants followed structured modules and published their emerging solutions; and third, as a site for feedback and evaluation from peers, facilitators, and subject matter experts.

Though the experiment used digital technology, it engaged people well beyond privileged global centers. For example, participants in South Africa's Free State, participating through StreetBiz's *Be a Nelson* Program, accessed tools and interacted using internet cafes. Refugees in Kenya's Kakuma camp, who participated via the HUBs program, interacted via mobile data packs. Belarussian participants took part via European Humanities University's university in exile. Students in countries facing ongoing war and repression, including Myanmar, Palestine, and Ukraine, took part through OSUN Online Courses.

The team also developed and employed a new competency framework, shown in Fig. 10, to look at the "muscle-building" that positions people to participate in building an experimental mindset.

Testing, Testing

During the period analyzed, all participants had access to the RebelBase platform. This provided step-by-step guidance for activities from prototyping and testing to competitive market analysis. Former participant Wei Jou Huang describes the program as "a system where every student can learn and grow by doing, by creating, by actually launching something" (Crawford & Plavin-Masterman, 2025c). As a 2023 participant in this forum through her university, Huang developed an experimental app to promote environmental awareness. She returned in 2024 as an alumni mentor for another project team. That team worked to take plastic waste littering the shores of Cox's Bazar, in Bangladesh, and turn it into filament for use in 3D printing applications.

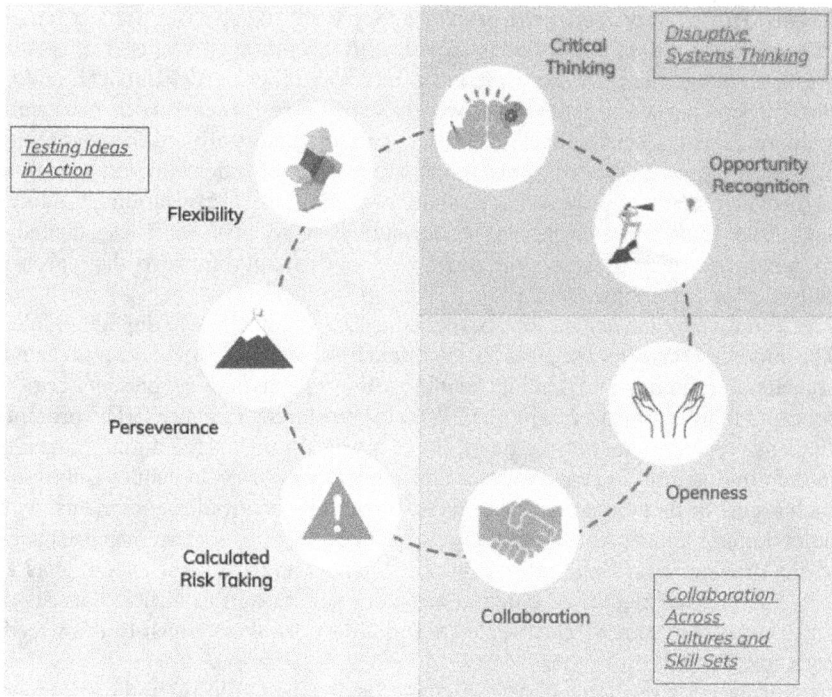

Fig. 10.   Competency Framework. *Source:* RebelBase, reprinted with
permission.

Huang emphasizes that the process teams follow makes creating an experimental solution *normal*. Referring to Tomás Mora of RebelBase, who co-created the forum and co-led the cohort in which she took part, she says "you can see that ... future you can actually build." This, Huang emphasizes, has a method to it, a set of steps. Through this method, "he [makes] it very normal to say, okay, you can go first step, second step, third step ... and in the end, you can build it. It's ... far beyond the courses ... a thing is possible to be built and to be solved, to be developed" (Crawford & Plavin-Masterman, 2025c).

Mora, for his part, emphasizes that participants like Huang create the journey; the method merely helps them reach the places they want to reach: "It's a learning path that is structured but flexible at the same time, which they can take in different directions [using] the same steps or similar steps. And whatever they find at the end,... it's their journey..." (Crawford & Plavin-Masterman, 2025c).

The community of practice developed a rigorous process and stuck to it, studying the results and refining the process each year. Participating organizations use a shared set of methodologies, assign participants to develop projects through asynchronous project assignments, and workshop results in shared weekly forums. Participants choose the problems they work to solve but use a common framework to build and present experimental solutions. Whatever a team's solution entails, the team must present it in a way other participants can understand, following a common set of weekly deliverables. Teams make their submissions digitally, get feedback from peers and instructors around the world, and modify in response. Weekly submissions, after being refined in this way, combine to form an integrated project. Each school or community organization has a local lead. The leads meet weekly to coordinate how to give feedback, facilitate constructive criticism from peers, and help participants improve their project deliverables in response.

To complete each deliverable, participants follow guidelines in digital modules. The modules serve as chapters in an interactive textbook for conceptualizing, launching, running, and scaling an innovation. Each module presents critical concepts followed by a prompt like "Who is your target audience?" The prompts challenge teams to answer the questions in a way that is unique and appropriate to their innovation. In response to each prompt, a project team defines and shares each aspect of its innovation, from its features to its financial requirements, with potential users, partners, resource providers, and others. The team then goes back to the drawing board and refines. In effect, teams improve their experiments as they conduct test flights on a digital airfield. In practice, this airfield consists of virtual space, structured methodology, and a network from which to draw feedback and support.

This network challenges participants to bridge their cultural and disciplinary backgrounds. Huang describes collaborating with a woman from Afghanistan, and the growth this collaboration fostered in both of them. Students from Europe and Asia, like herself, she says, are accustomed to working in online environments and using technical tools. They're used to sharing "our thoughts and experience(s)" and being "really honest to each other" (Crawford & Plavin-Masterman, 2025c). Her colleague in Afghanistan, by contrast, was in college when the Taliban took over and barred women from education. Huang says, "she's become very, very hopeless, but at the same time she's also trying to find some other way to learn and grow.... I can see her growth after this entire project ... through this collaboration series, kind of project-based developing.... It will have a real lasting effect throughout our life" (Crawford & Plavin-Masterman, 2025c).

The first two examples that follow illustrate projects launched using this process. The third example describes a new venture currently being developed by an entrepreneur *after* going through the process.

Rindco

The team behind Rindco Leathers did not start out assuming they'd win multiple competitive international grants for their fledgling venture. It was only when they made the top five teams in the program described above, that they began to think *they* might be people who could turn their idea into reality. Says CEO Shanen Anne Gomes:

> When we got selected for the top five final teams, we realized . . .
> this is an idea we should . . . look into and make it into a reality. . ..
> [E]verything about the course,. . . helped as a motivation. (Gomes
> Interview, 2025)

The team started simply trying to attack a system they thought worked badly
in their region.

> We saw that the production of leather, mainly from animal skin or
> PVC leather, [is] very harmful because . . . leather go[es] through a
> process called tanning, which uses harmful chemicals, which
> eventually get dumped into the rivers. And one of the biggest
> reasons for water pollution in Bangladesh is . . . tannery
> industries. So we thought fruit leather would be a very good
> alternative because it uses [few] chemicals in the tanning process.

The team also zeroed in on a second, related problem their product could
solve. Bangladesh generates large volumes of fruit peel as a byproduct of its
agricultural and food processing activities. Excess peel frequently gets discarded
as waste, creating both environmental and sanitation problems. Rindco aims to
alleviate the fruit peel waste problem in Bangladesh by upcycling this organic
material into high-quality, eco-friendly leather substitutes. Thus, Rindco began
with an experiment that linked two social/environmental problems: pollution
from leather production and waste from fruit consumption.

As the team conducted its field research, its members discovered that if it could
generate locally derived plant-based leather, it would also solve a significant
commercial problem. Through their professor (Sebastian Groh)'s connections, the
team met with Picard Bangladesh, a Bangladeshi leather goods exporter that
already faces significant demand for plant-based leather products. Picard
currently imports plant-based leather from the Americas, uses it to produce
handbags, belts, and shoes, and then ships the finished products *back* to Western
markets. A local source of plant-based leather could drive down the costs by
eliminating part of this back-and-forth journey.

The team's work to understand the commercial need led it to dig into a
technical problem – whether it could derive a plant-based bonding agent to glue
together strands of material derived from fruit peels "instead of using chemicals
for the bonding agent, because you can think of the fruit fibers as strings that you
need to just sew in to form the leather. So we obviously need a bonding agent to
get all the fibers.. . . In order to make it more sustainable . . . we are going to use
naturally sourced bonding agents from microorganisms called algae" (Gomes
Interview, 2025).

To develop the bonding agents, Gomes recruited a new team member who's
leading the algae testing. "We . . . know that algae produce biopolymers that can
act as good bonding agents. So . . . we need to . . . [determine] which species would
bond . . . best with which fruits, something that we are researching.. . . In the lab,

we are growing two algae species ... it takes around three to four weeks to totally cultivate the algae and [bring] it into a mature state" (Gomes Interview, 2025).

The team aims to have the first viable version of its product ready in 2025. "We hope that by ... this year, June [2025], we will have a Minimum Viable Product. At least we're hoping that by the end of the next month,... after growing [the algae] and adding to the fruit fiber, we will get ... an idea about the first two [strands], which can also help model the next four" (Gomes Interview, 2025).

To support development, the team has won three awards. One came through the program described here, a second through the H&M Foundation, and a third through a program called Unibator, run by the ICT Division of Bangladesh in collaboration with the World Bank.

Juan Lift

In the Philippines, Charnylle "Nylle" Antiporda is growing Juan Lift, a business aimed at training people with disabilities (PWDs) and placing them into jobs as virtual assistants around the world. He refined his idea in 2024 by participating in the process described above. His experience exhibits all four elements of the MDFC innovation model developed by Krskovo and Breyer: growth mindset (M), discipline (D), flow (F), and creativity (C) (Krskova & Breyer, 2023).

First, Antiporda practiced a *growth mindset* as he developed his project, incorporating new ideas along the way. He began with a general project description of using the digital economy to help orthopedically disabled people. After uploading his idea to the RebelBase platform, Antiporda says he received feedback on how to modify his approach to increase its chances of success. "[We got] feedback that ... [other participants] really cannot understand what our focus [is] on. So when I got an email from [a participant in the program named] Rachel, she discussed the different pros and cons of our project. And she mentioned that it's ... too broad to just say that we are going to digital. She [also] mentioned her experience as a virtual assistant" (Crawford & Plavin-Masterman, 2025b). In this way, Antiporda benefited from input from people he'd never met in person, who provided targeted and constructive critiques.

Second, he was *disciplined* – working with his local team and instructor, Ari Luis Halos, to conduct interviews and do market research. "[Professor] Ari ... is very supportive [of] us. He introduced different virtual agencies here in the Philippines, and ... we ... experienced interviewing them ... and we are able also to [under-stand] the issues that they are experiencing.... And we learned that they also offer trainings [*sic*] for people who have disabilities ... [but] there are no assurance[s] that these trained ... people are going to have a decent job. So that's [where] we want to fill the gap for Juan Lift" (Crawford & Plavin-Masterman, 2025b).

Antiporda drew specific lessons from these interviews with personnel at the virtual agencies about what it would take to bridge the gap for PWDs. "They ... mentioned that [people with disabilities] also struggles [*sic*] [with] being not technologically adept ... so ... for Juan Lift,... our goal is just to give sustainable work and opportunities for people who have disabilities" (Crawford & Plavin-Masterman, 2025b).

He was able to use his professor's feedback and local connections to interview stakeholders to understand where and how his placement and training agency fit into the competitive landscape. "We wanted to know what are the needs for our customers ... [so we] did ... surveys and interviews from PWD representatives, stakeholders, government agencies, NGOs for PWDs, and also for doctors and clinics... who will be our... customers [*sic*]" (Crawford & Plavin-Masterman, 2025b).

Third, the Juan Lift team reached deep into the ecosystem, drawing contributions from disparate collaborators. Their distinct skills and experiences came together, contributing to a shared experience of *flow* as the project took shape and built momentum. For example, Halos was able to find someone focused on indigenous training and placement in a similar field and set up a meeting with them as Antiporda continued to develop his idea. As Professor Halos explains, "we met with an entrepreneur who also has a VA, a virtual assistant agency. And she's from an Indigenous People group... and she's helping people in her tribe to become virtual assistants.... And... I thought that what she was doing for her tribe's people, ... becoming virtual assistants for people in the States, in Australia.... Maybe Nylle should have a conversation with her. And they actually met online" (Crawford & Plavin-Masterman, 2025b).

Finally, the team used a digital innovation ecosystem to feed their *creativity*. Juan Lift uses the digital space to enable PWDs in the Philippines to create and seize opportunities absent in the local economy. Antiporda even decided to focus on healthcare partially because of how much exposure the disabled have to healthcare and medical treatments. Bridging the limitations of physical remoteness, personal and professional background, and resource differences, the team was able to tap into the potential they already had for a growth mindset, discipline, flow, and creativity. Juan Lift is on its way. The company has trained and placed virtual assistants to help in healthcare settings in Australia, Asia, and the United States.[4]

Enthela

Bulgaria-based startup Enthela makes microbial bacteria that help keep more nitrogen in the soil, to provide "a sustainable and efficient alternative to nitrogen fertilizers" (Crawford & Plavin-Masterman, 2025a). The goal is to help farmers maintain soil fertility and yield while decreasing nitrogen fertilizer usage by up to 50%. Enthela is currently developing a proof of concept before going to market. To do so, cofounder Martin Nedev emphasizes, requires people whose specializations differ from his own. Nedev has a business background and needs to

---

[4]For a sampling of experiments, some of which will become established projects as they go through the funnel – and others of which will enable project teams to build capabilities along the way, see: https://app.rebelbase.co/browse

collaborate actively with scientists on his team. He didn't start out knowing how to work effectively with people across disciplinary and cultural backgrounds. Instead, he developed his capacity to do so through participation, in 2022, in the learning-by-doing program described above.

In the process, Nedev closed the distance between himself and collaborators whose experience diverged from his own. That divergence proved indispensable because the innovation happens across their combined skills and perspectives. To bridge the gap, Nedev needed to draw upon what he had learned in the 2022 program: "You ... [can] experience somebody else's problem who is really far away physically, but at the same time really close to you in terms of communication and in terms of knowledge. And we were able to see what are the problems from everywhere." As anyone who's been on countless video calls or message threads knows, that closeness doesn't always happen over digital media. The limits on traditional means for establishing rapport, from sharing meals to exchanging nonverbal trust cues, can make this particularly challenging. This may be especially true when people need to build bridges between different cultural and disciplinary backgrounds.

When Nedev was able to "experience somebody else's problem who is really far away physically, but at the same time really close to you in terms of communication" and "see what are the problems from everywhere," he built empathy. He asserts that this work across cultures and disciplines brings perspectives critical to solving emerging problems. "Our startup ecosystem in Europe, maybe in the States is the same, needs a little more diversity in terms of supporting people from different type[s] of groups, so they can work on their solution" (Crawford & Plavin-Masterman, 2025a).

In a deeply divided world, how is it possible that young people, interacting digitally, built empathy for others they'd never met in person, of backgrounds so different from their own? Through his participation in the 2022 program, Nedev got the chance to collaborate closely with people from distant places who brought training in unfamiliar disciplines. Their frames of reference diverged from his own. Despite these differences, empathy and camaraderie emerged *through* the process of digging into difficult, shared problems together. As participants worked to help improve each other's projects and experienced the kinds of flow and use of creativity Nylle describes, they gained empathy for people who might otherwise have seemed alien to them. Bridging these gaps, they learned to tackle knotty problems together – problems that had no "solution in the back of the book" – to develop experimental solutions to them.

It's one thing to empathize with people who remind you of yourself, or whose problems you relate to because you have experienced them directly. This book has documented the dangers of that approach. We've shown the risks of granting resources and opportunities to those who seem brilliant or courageous when they think like you do– who then build solutions that respond poorly to the needs of people whose needs differ from your own.

It's the Ecosystem

Nedev's former professor Van Mensel sees the connections participants make in the process as a game-changer:

> We can never underestimate the power of the network and how disadvantaged are those who don't have it.... One of the co-instructors in South Africa had to pay for access in an internet cafe for his cohort of aspiring entrepreneurs to be able to join our course ... through their mobile phones. For me, this is mind-blowing, I mean, hats off. And this is what we should be doing around the world. (Crawford & Plavin-Masterman, 2025a)

Problem solvers like Huang, Gomes, Antiporda, and Nedev don't start with resources and then develop their experiments. Instead, they conduct experiments that draw resources to them. They then refine those experiments based on the resources they marshal. Key resources include talent, qualified guidance, space to iterate with feedback, market information, and connections to potential partners. As these resources gather around emerging solutions, an innovation ecosystem takes shape. Conventionally, innovation ecosystems involve specific neighborhoods, physical meeting places, and resource providers. These innovators are now exploring the possibilities for an intersecting innovation ecosystem, one that spans localities. If we can build on their experience, we could open up the opportunity to innovate for many more people than have the ability today. To use Huang's term, we can make it "normal" to attempt to meet needs in new ways that normalize that, "a thing is possible to be built and to be solved, to be developed."

Often, the first resources innovators draw to them in the process are not financial. They take shape in sweat, partnerships, and opportunities that enable an experiment to evolve into a form that can in turn attract financial resources. Then a venture like Juan Lift can underwrite building out or purchasing tools, hiring people, and reaching its potential market. By investing in these things, the venture creates value that didn't exist before – in Antiporda's case, meaningful work opportunities for PWDs in the Philippines, valuable both to them and to those who hire them.

Referring to Nedev's experience, Van Mensel describes this as a journey – where having access to the chance to try is what counts. "Ideally, this becomes available to everyone in the world and doesn't have to be necessarily a student in a business school, in fact, someone who has to get funding to... get internet in an internet cafe, well, that person most definitely needs to have access to these tools that Martin Nedev had access to" (Crawford & Plavin-Masterman, 2025a).

These tools break the journey into guided steps: "They have access to the platform and they look at it and they say, step number one, I have to first do my marketing research right now to get... out of the building, speak to some people and see if there's a market for this idea..." (Crawford & Plavin-Masterman, 2025a). She describes this as a journey that opens up the possibility of drawing more resources: "those innovations that we talk about ... are going to change the world. They take time, they take a lot of money, they are [a] huge risk. But if we don't embark on this journey, then we also never stand a chance" (Crawford & Plavin-Masterman, 2025a). This differs markedly from a top-down approach that tries to pick winners and allocate funds directly to them. Antiporda, Gomes, Nedev, and Huang may or may not succeed in the particular experiments, but they become people who know how to conduct experiments. This can be quantified.

Survey Says

Over four years, the team studying participants' experience tested a central hypothesis: *the act of building experiments through a structured process cultivates the experimental mindset.* The team broke the mindset down into three broad "domains" of capabilities. These domains include disruptive systems thinking, collaboration across cultures and skill sets, and testing ideas in action. Together, the domains comprise the competency framework pictured in Fig. 10.

This framework, developed by Crawford, Tuba Erbil, and Thomas Gold, attempts to assess the potential of a range of participants to attack broken systems with new ideas, work on multifunctional/diverse teams, and pitch others on emerging experiments.

Participants came from a range of levels and backgrounds, including:

- Science students like Gomes and Huang, and those pursuing engineering and law, like Gomes' team members.
- Entrepreneurs with technology backgrounds, like Nedev, and entrepreneurship students like Antiporda.
- MBAs and EMBAs like Groh's students.
- Nonstudents interested in building experiments, such as StreetBiz's "Nelsons."

To allow for the range of experience levels and backgrounds, the team assessed both the skill level retained (if participants started high) and gained (if they moved from low to high).

After participants submitted their experiments using the RebelBase modules and updated them to complete their projects, they completed anonymous surveys. These surveys assessed whether this model was effective in building capacity for the experimental mindset. They also included questions about hard skills, like formulating a theory of change, competitive analysis, or financial projections; and soft skills, like thinking critically about systems that don't work, or finding opportunities to derive solutions in the face of tricky problems. Analysis of aggregate survey results yielded insights about activities combining such hard and soft skills, for example: learning to pitch an emerging idea to others who can help realize it in practice by bringing skills, resources, or opportunities. The study also provided insights into participants' interaction with others – and how they collaborate with people from other disciplines and cultural backgrounds in developing a new experiment.

This research suggests that an experimental mindset may be addictive – and that people learn to do it by doing it. Over four years, the vast majority of respondents reported that they gained or retained skills in critical thinking (86%) and opportunity recognition – seeing an opening where others might see barriers (85%). Participants also reported gaining or maintaining openness on diverse teams (89%) and gaining or maintaining capabilities to collaborate on diverse teams – forging connections with others and improving their capacity to bring diverse skills and backgrounds to produce innovative thinking in a group or on a team (85%).

These aggregate results provide quantitative insights into the qualitative observations participants offered during the interviews we presented above.

Participants reported improving or maintaining their capacity to test and refine ideas. This included the ability to take risks and understand the risks they were taking (83%), the ability to persevere in the face of failure or setback (82%), and flexibility, or being able to modify an idea or approach when given constructive feedback (81%). Table 1 shows aggregate survey results from 2020 to 2023.

Table 1. RebelBase Survey Responses, 2020–2023.

Domain	(a) % of Respondents Who Report an Increase in Scores	(b) % of Respondents Who Report Consistent High Scores	(c) ((a) + (b)) Increase or Retained Level %
Critical Thinking and Opportunity Recognition			
Critical thinking	52%	34%	86%
Opportunity recognition	62%	23%	85%
Openness and Collaboration on Diverse Teams			
Openness	45%	44%	89%
Collaboration	42%	43%	85%
Testing and Refining Ideas in Action			
Calculated risk-taking	64%	20%	83%
Perseverance	50%	32%	82%
Flexibility	46%	35%	81%

Source: RebelBase, with permission.

Note: 392 responses out of 855 surveys sent, for a response rate of 46%. See Appendix for methodology.

Expanding the Surface Area

In Chapter 12, we introduced Scott Anthony's notion of serendipity surface area, and its relationship to both individual initiative and ecosystem access. The results of Crawford and company's research suggest that a structured process, for deriving solutions for which there is no blueprint, gives people practice at being persistent and resourceful, even when it takes repeated trials and failures. This aligns with the MDFC model, which argues that "when discipline is applied to increase focus, the flow state – the essential ingredient of enhanced creativity (or the cornerstone of innovation) – can be improved" (Krskova & Breyer, 2023, p. 8). Krskova and Breyer emphasize that this model can *enhance capacity for innovation* in traditional spheres like business, and across activities: "The [MDFC] model is suitable for individuals wishing to embrace thinking outside of the box to reap the benefits of enhancing their capacity for innovation in all aspects of their lives" (Krskova & Breyer, 2023, p. 8).

This is the "how" of Steve Jobs' "most important thing." Today, Jobs' notion of empowering people to take on Goliath and reshape the world can seem hopelessly naive in the face of venture capital's inbred coziness, dominant firms' power consolidation, and the spread of models and systems unresponsive to either the global polycrisis or the everyday crises of navigating life in cattle class. Still, when we listen to what young people like Huang, Gomes, Antiporda, and Nedev describe, Jobs' idea holds surprising power today.

Apple's famous *Think Different* campaign legendarily ran these two words above portraits of people who embodied Jobs' ethos that imaginative people can reshape the world. In one spot, Nelson Mandela smiles out at us, seeming to brim with possibility, his chin framed by his fingers. Social entrepreneur Nico de Klerk launched South Africa's StreetBiz Foundation to honor Mandela's legacy by developing a social entrepreneurship mindset among youth. Calling this the "Be a Nelson" movement, de Klerk frames Mandela's power as *making the seemingly impossible possible*. Entrepreneurs based out of the South African townships work on new solutions alongside Sebastian Groh's business students in Bangladesh. In an article for OSUN called "Who Shapes the Future," one of the authors quotes de Klerk, who points out that all people have a role in building the future. "To approach the world the way Mandela did is to change it from a given – that we must operate within – to something we're actively creating – and to change who we think has the chance to create."

This begs a crucial question: "'Can we learn to enable the people who are closest to the problems so they can generate the novel solutions they need?' For the global community of 'co-instructors' of which de Klerk is a member, the answer is simple: we must" (Crawford, 2023). To democratize innovation will be difficult, but the costs of failing to do so are incalculable – and early results suggest that the energy for it is already present, waiting to be channeled. The research presented here deserves to be followed by larger, more longitudinal studies that go beyond participant self-assessment. We need wider tests of the hypothesis that the experimental mindset can be learned by doing – and that if we use technology differently, we have unprecedented capacity to expand who gets to build experiments of their own. If participant surveys from experimental programs tell us anything, it's that to build responsive systems for tomorrow, we must broaden *who* gets to innovate. We must open up the chance to experiment, beyond those who move through the same few institutions, come from the same demographics, or share similar frames of reference.

To do so would constitute a major paradigm shift. The mechanics of funding so often look for the direct effect, within a limited time period, and fail to account for ripple effects. They aim to provide something directly to a target population and tally the results that generates. If our demonstrations are any indication, that approach falls short, because resilience develops through building the capacity to create solutions from the ground up. What would it take to build an economy of resilience, fueled by waves of experimentation beyond the same old folks?

Chapter 14

Launch a Bottom-Up Revolution

What We're Up Against

Unresponsive systems have come to dominate much of modern life. Everywhere we turn – healthcare, food, travel, banking, education – we face such systems in our work and as consumers. Strive as we might to escape life in cattle class, many of us feel that our way of life is under attack. When an unresponsive system encroaches on us, most of the time that system lacks a clear face. We can vent our anger at the call center employee on the other end of the phone, but how satisfying is that, really?

For many, there's a creeping sense that the life you expected or aspired to is slipping further from your grasp. Against this backdrop, anger against out-groups erupts in country after country, while crises seem to pile up wherever you turn: natural disasters and pandemics; terrorist attacks and waves of refugees; social and economic disruptions of all kinds (Muis & Reeskens, 2021). Clouds from the far-away wildfire linger overhead. Migrants from hotter parts of the world gather at borders. Add grievances against the growing frustrations of everyday life, throw in a liberal amount of desperation for someone to blame, and you've got a vicious cycle. As the polycrisis intensifies, new waves of people seek somewhere safer. As they do, outrage and grievance grow. Grievance triggers more grievance, until for many of us, it becomes our default state.

Business as Usual

When you hear someone bragging about how efficient they're going to make things, consider the price. There's no such thing as a free flywheel or hockey stick. The next time you find yourself stuck in the predictable doom loop or screaming into the void, it may feel like it's just you. It's not. The coming story might not involve Boeing or United Healthcare, but it will soon make the news – you can count on that. The next crisis you experience personally is coming, too. It might not be a hospital losing you or a loved one in the system. It might not be the latest global climate conference coming to nothing worth writing home about, but the next storm is brewing. When it wreaks its havoc, leaders everywhere will express

One Size Fits None, 135–142
Copyright © 2025 Alejandro Juárez Crawford and Miriam Plavin-Masterman
Published under exclusive licence by Emerald Publishing Limited
doi:10.1108/978-1-83608-660-420251015

commiseration. Few of them will connect the dots – or if they do, they'll connect the wrong ones.

Life in cattle class is the price we pay for the never-ending pursuit of "efficient" models across industries and governments. We subsidize these models every time we tolerate an unresponsive system. Despite the vision we're often sold of lives enhanced by automation, the capacity to understand and respond to our needs becomes increasingly reserved for premium options.

The cost to us of putting up with unresponsive systems is more unresponsive systems. The cost to the economy and society is that our systems become brittle and slow to change, just when our opportunity lies in reinventing the way things work. Even as crises burn through our lives – from the unaffordability of essential goods in markets dominated by a few large players to the latest region wiped out by flood or fire – we fail to build responsive systems.

Climate change serves as a force multiplier. If we fail to transform the global economy in the next decade, it will affect everything else. Given that limited runway, it's tempting to seek the big fix. But the riskiest thing we can do now is trust "the best and the brightest" to get us out of this jam when few of them face the problems the rest of us face. Shower opportunities and resources for experimentation on the privileged few; end up with one-size-fits-none solutions.

Could we instead create a flywheel, not for taking a given model to megascale, but instead for generating many diverse models, each of which responds to particular needs, often in innovative ways? This book documents the power it unleashes when people get opportunities to practice building solutions. Now comes the larger task of opening widespread access to Kitty Hawks for today's version of those bike mechanics of old.

To do so requires that we change the way we think. It's also eminently practical. It takes advantage of the resourcefulness with which human beings have always created solutions to the problems we face. We have the technology. We can make space for everyday innovators to create thousands of locally responsive solutions. This lies within our reach. We can give people who imagine things working differently, in their communities and for the planet, the chance to attempt experiments of their own. To release their energies, we must broaden access to the chance to learn, by doing, to remake the way things work. In this way, we can create systems that meet our needs, from how we treat our ailments to how we get the clothes we wear.

The process for achieving this will be decentralized, messy – and necessary. We can begin by linking what already exists, connecting organizations – including community groups, schools, and companies ready to invest in innovation from the bottom up – to form intersecting ecosystems. The previous chapter shows the power it unleashes when we do this using shared innovation infrastructure. It's time to expand upon this widely, to equip and connect the wave of innovators we now need. The energy for this wave is there, waiting, ready to gain momentum.

Go back to the young Steve Jobs looking up one of the HP founders in the phone book. Before the digital age, the network of resources, relationships, and institutions that make up an innovation ecosystem had to develop *locally*. Today, local problems and stakeholders remain essential. Unlike when Hewlett or Jobs was coming up, however, you don't need to go to the same coffee shop, or even be in the same city, to share an innovation ecosystem. Tech can connect you to an innovation ecosystem beyond where you live or work. When you look at the way things work today and think "What if instead …?" you can find the tools and collaborators you need to develop an experiment of your own, take part in an experiment, or support one. This could become normal.

Innovator's Infrastructure

Matthew Barzun paraphrases Sherry Turkle: "Technology has given us independence – freedom from hassles and wires and other people's choices – and more efficient lives, but it has largely broken its promise to give us freedom with one another to build big things together" (Barzun, 2021). Why has tech so far failed to fulfill this promise?

As we saw in the last chapter, you develop the mindset for creating new solutions by attempting to create new solutions. This involves working with others from different backgrounds, who provide collaboration, resources, and opportunities. A flywheel for generating many experiments needs an infrastructure that connects people to the space, tools, and resources to develop solutions.

How does an *emerging* solution or *evolving* experiment find those who can add talent, resources, advice, opportunities, partnerships, and other crucial inputs to it? When the main obstacle to creating value is enabling counterparts to find each other and connect, it's called a "two-sided market problem." Traditionally, platforms solve such problems by getting users on each side to reveal characteristics relevant to their counterparts, and then matching those users with each other. This works well when users can create, for example, employment or dating profiles featuring the characteristics relevant for matching. However, creating a new solution is not as simple as submitting a job application or using a dating app. Enabling potential innovators to find each other and connect productively presents at least four challenges:

(1) *Evolving Shape:* The solution's characteristics evolve.
(2) *Emerging Skills:* A person who can create part of a solution (such as a product design) often lacks the skills to develop other components (like financial projections).
(3) *Feedback Loop:* Innovators need to test aspects of an emerging solution with team members and mentors, in workshops, and through field research.
(4) *Proprietary Components:* Experimenters can be concerned about sharing their solutions, because they don't feel ready, or worry others will copy what they've developed.

Solving the two-sided market problem for innovators requires addressing each of these challenges. Innovators learn from their markets and users, then pivot as needed. Entrepreneurs draw capabilities to their innovations to help them take shape. Feedback loops often power the programs that serve such innovators and entrepreneurs. The fourth challenge – sharing solutions – can be sensitive. There are times when an innovator needs to protect a proprietary recipe, formula, algorithm, or design. When investment in innovation depends upon dominating markets and consolidating industries, innovators may hold their cards especially close to their vests. For people solving problems in their respective locales, however, much can be learned by comparing notes (to Shuman's point). Indeed, entrepreneurs often create value by introducing variations and modifications that work well for local needs, as Jane Jacobs stresses.

The innovators we quote in the last chapter describe a process that guides them and a web of people who help them. Taking the leap becomes "normal," to use Huang's term, when she knows the steps and can find the help she needs. That's innovation infrastructure in action. If we can furnish frontline organizations with such infrastructure, we can create a wider innovation ecosystem. We can enable talented innovators to solve problems in places where we need innovation, rather than forcing them to move to global centers to have a chance of accessing what they need. As Shuman emphasizes, for the local economy to be successful, it needs to be powered by local businesses. Against a backdrop of expanding one-size-fits-none models, someone needs to be in a position to start the local business.

To help local problem-solvers, frontline organizations need innovation infrastructure that addresses each of the four challenges listed above. As the research we present in the last chapter suggests, this infrastructure should include:

- guidance for developing a solution and communicating each part of it;
- tools enabling people with various skills to collaborate on the solution;
- virtual spaces for gaining feedback and refining each aspect of the solution; and
- control over which pieces of the solution get shared, and with whom.

These inputs help the innovator shape a solution into a form that can attract resources and build their capacity for successive experiments. Still, this list is not meant to be exhaustive. We hope that readers of this book will refine and expand on it after conducting further experiments – both through experiments solving problems around them and by developing programs that enable more people to do so. The research and examples we have presented suggest that we can bridge the gap. Bridging it enables a far wider range of institutions to open up an innovation ecosystem for the people they serve.

A Network of Networks: For People Creating Experiments of Their Own

After working through the modules we describe in Chapter 13, Shanen Gomes of Rindco applied to various opportunities for innovators and entrepreneurs, gaining resources and further chances to experiment. Such opportunities exist all over the world, offered by a range of "frontline" organizations. For example, innovation, social impact, and entrepreneurship centers serve universities, companies, and communities. Such centers can become nodes in a web connecting aspiring innovators with wider access to what they need. Each node brings resources – including talent, capabilities, and facilities – relevant to problems and opportunities across the network. Nodes also contribute data, methods, and examples to inform work across industries and regions.

University and community-based programs often provide legitimacy to the aspiring innovator, which can prove critical in a search for funding. Sometimes, universities can join consortia of organizations, whether local, regional, or global. Chambers of commerce, community-based organizations, foundations, and local governments also have roles to play. Local foundations and nonprofit organizations often provide grants for community-led projects, including but not limited to educational campaigns, green infrastructure development, and food security programs. In an advanced scenario, more of these independent programs could be connected to global talent and resource providers in a global network.

Consider a few examples of existing programs that could both add to and benefit from a shared innovation infrastructure. In many cases, existing programs are both regional and topical in their focus. That's the case in these examples, which feature organizations and consortia in Europe and North America, focused on seeding climate solutions through grants, and in some cases technical assistance. We introduce them in part to help frame the challenge. What could we achieve if this kind of infrastructure were available well beyond the Global North, on local terms? How much power would it unleash if we could connect efforts like these, with their regional and topical focus, using innovation infrastructure the way Antiporda, Huang, Gomes, and Nedev describe it?

In 2020, the International Council for Local Environmental Initiatives (ICLEI) Europe launched the ICLEI Action Fund (supported by Google) to support European nonprofits and academic institutions tackling climate action. In the ICLEI case, organizations must use data and technology in their climate projects. Between 2020 and 2024, the ICLEI fund gave out over 10 million Euros to finance 16 climate projects (ICLEI Europe Action Fund).

In the Northeastern United States, the University of Connecticut (UCONN)'s Connecticut Institute for Resilience and Climate Adaptation (CIRCA), in collaboration with the Connecticut Department of Energy and Environmental Protection (DEEP), is distributing grants "for projects that increase the capacity of vulnerable communities to mitigate, plan for, and respond to climate change impacts. . . . [Funding is available for] community-based organizations, [Native American] tribal governments, and tribal organizations to support planning, capacity-building, or education projects that advance community-scale climate adaptation and/or climate mitigation efforts" (Buchanan, 2022).

The Great Lakes Integrated Sciences and Assessment (GLISA) serves Illinois, Indiana, Michigan, Minnesota, New York, Ohio, Pennsylvania, and Wisconsin in the United States, along with the Province of Ontario in Canada. Since 2011, GLISA has competitively awarded 42 small grants of up to $35,000 each to local and regional organizations committed to using climate information to support adaptation. Funded organizations work with GLISA (and its researchers from the

University of Wisconsin, University of Michigan, and Michigan State University) to advance climate adaptation throughout North America's Great Lakes region (GLISA, n.d.).

In Washington State, the statewide Department of Commerce provides grants and technical assistance to cities and counties working to plan for climate change. The department offered approximately $30 million in statewide grants for the 2023–2025 grant period, with counties eligible for grants between $300,000 and $800,000 and cities eligible for grants between $100,000 and $700,000 (Washington State Department of Commerce, 2024). On a smaller scale, the local town council in Surrey, England, is launching a climate action fund, with grants of up to £5,000 available for individuals and groups tackling climate change locally. Projects must be community-driven to qualify. These grants fund projects that "focus on education around carbon emissions, biodiversity enhancement, energy, water, and waste reduction" (Panons, 2024).

Shared innovation infrastructure could widen the funnel of innovators eligible for opportunities like these, by guiding, equipping, and connecting small groups and individuals creating solutions. It could also connect innovators funded through programs in one part of the world to partners elsewhere. When people working on related problems bring much-needed insights, capabilities, and resources, it solves the two-sided market problem for innovators and entrepreneurs. It also enables local problem-solvers to learn from and build on each other's efforts in the way Shuman describes.

The examples we've just given focus on the Global North, where states, municipalities, and corporate donors are often relatively well-resourced. To put the grant amounts in these examples into perspective, current estimates are that less than 2% of philanthropic funding is currently dedicated to addressing climate change. In the United States, grants for climate change continue to represent a small fraction of all giving (estimated at 2–3%). At one point in the 2020s, funding rose "60% for combatting super-pollutants,... likely boosted by more than 20 philanthropies launching the Global Methane Pledge in late 2020 and committing $328 million to reducing [methane] emissions" (Climate Change Grants for Nonprofits | Inside Philanthropy, n.d.).

There's no shortage of capital in the world. Can connecting local programs like these through shared innovator's infrastructure bring more resources into play? Can we do this not only for innovators in the Global North but for a wide range of people facing the worst impacts of climate change?

Let's Dance

An entrepreneurial revolution depends upon empowering people close to problems who could, given half a chance, create a wave of experiments. Do enough people have the necessary motivation and grit? "Individuals need to have the willingness to try to do something new, even if it can result in failure" (Krskova & Breyer, 2023, p. 8). The research we have presented strongly suggests that this mindset can be developed. In the surveys of innovators from a range of backgrounds using the RebelBase platform, many respondents rated themselves as starting out with low levels of risk-taking and opportunity recognition. *People don't have to begin with an experimental mindset to develop solutions. They develop an experimental mindset by building solutions.*

Given the chance to practice the mindset we've described, people from a range of backgrounds collaborate on experimental solutions and learn to attract resources to them. The resourcefulness and shared agency they exhibit can be honed through the right kinds of *practice*. Then "ecosystems grow around them, attracting networks of talent and expanding access to skills and resources for promising experiments" (Crawford et al., 2023).

Though more longitudinal research is needed, the data we have presented suggest that the process of taking risks and looking for opportunities *builds* the capacity to take good risks – and forges the connections that power an ecosystem. Think of something as simple as a dance floor. At the beginning of a party, the floor is empty. Perhaps one dancer, who seems to lack inhibitions, dances alone for a while. For most people at the party, the empty dance floor remains intimidating. Then something changes. A few people get excited about a song and start to lose themselves in interactions with each other. Those interactions make it possible for others to take a risk and join the dance. Suddenly, for many more people, it's easy to join in.

We all recognize this phenomenon when it comes to dancing, but seem to have forgotten how it applies to the economy. If the experiments we present in the previous chapter demonstrate anything, it is that it is now possible to open up the "dance floor" of entrepreneurship and innovation if we're creative enough in how we use digital tools. Ask a group of people of any age, anywhere in the world, whether they see themselves as entrepreneurs, and you might get some hands. Ask them what should work differently in their communities or industries, or the world, and virtually all have answers. Open up a structured opportunity to conduct experiments into how things might work, with support along the way, and something magical happens. Majorities embrace the opportunity, emerge with powerful skills and a more experimental mindset, and come back asking for more. Can we expand access to this opportunity quickly enough, so that enough people in enough places can invent a future that responds to their needs, one in which they can thrive?

To have a shot, we need to use every tool at our disposal to make it possible for those who haven't yet had the chance to innovate to do so. Only they can develop the models we need to overhaul industries and economies from the bottom up. It's time to use our digital commons to make sure the best of our talent gets the chance to shape the future on their terms, for all of our sakes.

There's no single formula for how problem-solvers draw resources like money, talent, and partnerships to their experiments. Still, the process itself generates momentum. Through this process, innovators learn to draw resources to their experiments. We need to expand access to it, and at the same time get better at bringing new resource providers into contact with the experiments that result, the solutions they offer, and the people who launch them. A two-sided market problem can't be solved from just one side.

No Hollywood hero is riding in to save us, but we have the technology to open up the chance to mount expeditions. We need many experiments since we don't know where each one will lead. Our dominant institutions – banks, governments, consultancies, private equity firms, and VCs – often hinder the development of responsive models, in all the ways we describe in this book. A few "genius" innovations won't build the global innovation ecosystem we now need. One size fits none. Instead of offering a few efficient recipes, it's time to try out many recipes and see what we can cook up.

The Opening

One person doesn't make a revolution, but many people, experimenting and communicating, can. Steve Jobs picked up the phone and called Hewlett. Today, we can make it possible for folks on every continent, with knowledge of local needs and ideas for how things could work differently, to give their ideas a try. The research we've presented shows the energy exists, if we open up channels for it.

To do so, we've got to shift our paradigm. We keep looking for the one big fix, and here we are. Charlie Brown's got to stop trying to kick that football.

This phase of the digital age will take us in one direction or the other. We can slide toward more top-down automation, with all the unresponsiveness that comes with it. Or we can use digital tools to equip and connect people as they launch experiments, far beyond the traditional centers the World Economic Forum calls "innovation-driven economies" (Global Entrepreneurship Monitor, 2024). Many problem solvers, in a far wider range of places, can then spin webs of resilience as they shape a future responsive to the needs of everyday people.

The power resident in many piecemeal experiments can be hard to see clearly. Successful experiments take place along with many failures and mixed results. There's no one hero in the story. Still, the opening is right there if we're willing to recognize it and take it. We can begin a new era in which launching experiments of our own becomes as normal as watching videos on our phones. If four years of working with young people on five continents has shown anything, this is not as crazy as it sounds. People in all environments are already doing it, often against the odds. An entrepreneurial revolution has begun. Let's take the opening we've got.

Appendix: Survey Research Design and Methodology Summary

Goals of the Study: The primary objective of this ongoing study is to evaluate skills and mindset built through project-based learning (PBL) and explore the scalability of such learning globally, using a shared digital platform. The broader ambition is to understand what it takes to equip individuals to tackle systemic issues through live experiments and social innovation.

Study Design: The study employed a structured PBL approach, in which participants from global cohorts developed projects to solve real-world problems through a series of modules on the RebelBase platform. Participants focused on developing solutions, refining them through feedback, and presenting cohesive final projects. The program followed a practicum model, including weekly peer critiques and workshops to support continuous project improvement.

Project-Based Format: Participants collaborated globally to work on social and environmental challenges, such as reducing waste and developing financial models for rural farmers. Each week, they submitted project components for feedback from instructors and peers, refining their work. This collaborative format fostered diverse perspectives and standardized the experiential learning process across geographical regions.

Competency Framework: Three broad competency domains were evaluated using surveys with retrospective questions:

(1) *Disruptive Systems Thinking* – Participants' ability to critically analyze existing systems and identify opportunities for change.
(2) *Collaboration Across Cultures and Skill Sets* – The capacity to collaborate on diverse teams, integrating perspectives and skills to solve problems.
(3) *Testing Ideas in Action* – How well participants took calculated risks, demonstrated perseverance, and exhibited flexibility in adapting their solutions.

Research Methodology: Surveys were administered anonymously after program completion. By asking participants to assess their level before and after participation, survey questions aimed to capture participants' self-assessed growth in skills such as critical thinking, collaboration, and entrepreneurial problem-solving.

The study's outcomes provide insights into how PBL, combined with a global, collaborative digital platform, can foster the development of entrepreneurial and social innovation skills and mindset on a global scale.

References

Aaron, N. (2024, January 18). Why most Netflix movies are so bad. https://shorturl.at/pXM8v

Accenture. (2022, November 1). Nearly all companies will miss net zero goals without at least doubling rate of carbon emissions reductions by 2030, Accenture report finds. https://shorturl.at/vJUDJ

Acemoglu, D. (2021, May 20). AI's future doesn't have to be dystopian. *Boston Review*. https://shorturl.at/DS1Oq

Adams, D. (1979). *Hitchhiker's guide to the galaxy*. Pan Books.

Adams, D. (2002). *The salmon of doubt: Hitchhiking the galaxy one last time*. Pan Books.

Adams, J. (2002, January 29). US venture capital investment dropped 65% in 2001. *Financial News*. https://tinyurl.com/3ab84ujm

Alvarado-Quesada, C. (2024, July 26). *Immigration does not start at the US border*. Project Syndicate. https://tinyurl.com/6va5uf2v

Anderson, S. (2023, August 11). Governments plan massive expansion of fossil fuel production despite climate crisis, UN warns. *Health Policy Watch*. https://tinyurl.com/4w7xezt6

Anderson, K. (2023, October 30). The wealth factor: The role of rich people in climate change. https://tinyurl.com/3wjpuuuk

Anthony, S. (2024, August 15). *Scott D. Anthony on LinkedIn: Scott Anthony AOM serendipity presentation*. Linkedin. https://tinyurl.com/4p2bh62e

APCO. (2023, November 29). *Climate change is top global concern, public expects transparency on climate action*, APCO Survey Finds.

Audia, P. G., & Rider, C. I. (2005). A garage and an idea: What more does an entrepreneur need? *California Management Review, 48*(1), 6–28. https://doi.org/10.2307/41166325

Barzun, M. (2021). *The power of giving away power: How the best leaders learn*. Random House. https://tinyurl.com/yr9xe8zk

Beer, S. (2002). What is cybernetics? *Kybernetes, 31*(2), 217. https://doi.org/10.1108/03684920210417283

Benjamin, D., & Komlos, D. (2021, September 13). The purpose of a system is what it does, not what it claims to do. *Forbes*. https://tinyurl.com/yntmvav5

Beres, D., & Warzel, C. (2024, May 8). Watch Apple trash-compact human culture. *The Atlantic*. https://tinyurl.com/mr2twm9m

Berger, J. (1972). *Ways of seeing* (2nd ed.). BBC and Penguin Books.

Bhanu, T. (2023, September 14). 16 leading companies using chatbots for customer service. *SiteGPT*. https://tinyurl.com/yw8db2ks

Bittle, J. (2023, December 5). Inside the Marshall Islands' life-or-death plan to survive climate change. *Grist*. https://tinyurl.com/vu5uv7k8

Black, S., Liu, A. A., Parry, I., & Vernon, N. (2023). *IMF fossil fuel subsidies data: 2023 update.* https://tinyurl.com/57e545h3

Borenstein, S. (2025, January 10). Earth breaks yearly heat record and lurches past dangerous warming threshold. *Associated Press News.* https://shorturl.at/WNmDX

Bourdieu, P. (1986). The forms of capital. In J. Richardson (Ed.), *Handbook of theory and research for the sociology of education* (pp. 241–258). Greenwood.

Bourdieu, P., & Passeron, J.-C. (1990). *Reproduction in education, society and culture* R. Nice, Trans. (2nd ed.). Sage Publications, Inc.

Brown, A. (2017, September 19). 100 quotes on business from the 100 greatest living business minds. *Forbes.* https://tinyurl.com/4wv7pds5

Brush, S. (2024, December 19). *BlackRock writes down flagship renewable fund, overhauls leaders.* Bloomberg. https://tinyurl.com/5hfzdxaj

Buchanan, M. (2022, October 11). *Climate and equity grant program.* Connecticut Institute for Resilience & Climate Adaptation (CIRCA). https://tinyurl.com/3m7jzzus

Buehler, N. (2023, June 28). How Coca-Cola makes money. Blog: *Investopedia.* https://tinyurl.com/33swbtaf

Butler, D. (2021, August 6). Turkey spent only fraction of forest protection budget before wildfires erupted. *Reuters.* https://tinyurl.com/2swufum4

Byrne, D. (2024, May 7). How artificial intelligence is helping Ghana plan for a renewable energy future. *Nature.* https://tinyurl.com/bd3svdx5

Caballero, R. (2008). Creative destruction. In L. E. Blume & S. N. Durlauf (Eds.), *The new Palgrave dictionary of economics* (2nd ed., pp. 1–5). Springer Nature. https://tinyurl.com/37jvrt9r

Camilleri, A. R., & Larrick, R. P. (2015). Choice architecture. In *Emerging trends in the social and behavioral sciences.* John Wiley & Sons, Inc. https://tinyurl.com/yc2f7xy3

Capolaghi, L. (2021, September 22). European venture capital's resilience through a global pandemic. *EY Luxembourg.* https://tinyurl.com/bdcvuhps

Carr, N. (2021, May 25). What the Silicon Valley idealists got wrong. *Engelsberg Ideas.* https://tinyurl.com/5abu4r25

Carroll, L. (2010). Through the looking glass, and what Alice found there. https://tinyurl.com/ty2bx4tn

Catherine. (2021, April 12). Number of business consulting firms in the world. *Wonder.* https://tinyurl.com/2cnjhyea. Accessed on July 17, 2024.

CGEP. (2019). Energy and development in a changing world: A framework for the 21st century. https://tinyurl.com/y6rtaykz

Chaffey, D. (2024, May). Global social media statistics research summary 2024. https://tinyurl.com/yp57byjv

Chancel, L. (2022, September 29). Global carbon inequality over 1990–2019. *Nature.* https://tinyurl.com/3pcsxfts

Christensen, C. (2012, March 30). *Disruptive innovation explained.* Video recording. https://tinyurl.com/bdfmhj6y

Climate Analytics and New Climate Institute. (2023). 2100 Warming projections: Emissions and expected warming based on pledges and current policies. Climate Action Tracker (2023). https://tinyurl.com/4prnbhz

Cohan, W. D. (2022, November 21). Opinion | How one of the country's most storied C.E.O.s destroyed his legacy. *The New York Times.* https://tinyurl.com/52j277df

Coherent Market Insights. (2021). Global climate change consulting market is estimated to account for US$ 8,653.7 mn by end of 2028, says coherent market insights (CMI). *Global Newswire*. https://tinyurl.com/mw4vhnmx

Corporate Europe Observatory. (December 19, 2023). "COP28 facilitates fossil fuel frenzy." Corporate Europe Observatory. Wrap-Up blog from UN Climate Summit (blog). https://tinyurl.com/39t22xfc

Craig, D. (2005). *Rip-off! The scandalous inside story of the management consulting money machine* (1st ed.). The Original Book Company.

Crawford, A. J. (2022, April 26). Equipping students to build the vital institutions that autocrats hate by Alejandro Juárez Crawford. *Rooted Resources*. https://tinyurl.com/2my8x5fx

Crawford, A. J. (2023, December 4). Who shapes the future? Extending the certificate in sustainability & social enterprise to individuals building community Ventures in South Africa. https://tinyurl.com/9sfmyeua

Crawford, A. J., & Plavin-Masterman, M. (2024a, April 10). Own what you want to do | A conversation with Dr. Andrews Ayiku (1) (Broadcast), https://tinyurl.com/469xspx7. Accessed on August 28, 2024.

Crawford, A. J., & Plavin-Masterman, M. (2024b, June 14). A hundred thousand small experiments | A conversation with Dr. Sebastian Groh (5) (Broadcast). https://tinyurl.com/2939j8n3. Accessed on August 28, 2024.

Crawford, A. J., & Plavin-Masterman, M. (2024c, July 4). Everyone is living in different parts of the world, but there's something that attached us all together | A conversation with Dalia Najjar (7) (Broadcast). https://tinyurl.com/7dm7jmpa

Crawford, A. J., & Plavin-Masterman, M. (2024d, August 22). A system where local is the norm – and we pay what it really costs to drive something hundreds of miles | A conversation with Trevor Vaughn and Hunter Buffington (11) (Broadcast). https://tinyurl.com/f7ed5t3j

Crawford, A. J., & Plavin-Masterman, M. (2024e, August 22). Talking to people who think like us has made us stagnant | A conversation with Trevor Vaughn and Hunter Buffington (10) (Broadcast). https://tinyurl.com/mwfntzpm

Crawford, A. J., & Plavin-Masterman, M. (2024f, September 5). It's a broken system | A conversation with David Benzaquen (12) (Broadcast). https://tinyurl.com/yc3r5pks

Crawford, A. J., & Plavin-Masterman, M. (2025a, February 25). Mentorship & collaboration: The alignment that changes the world | A conversation with Evelina Van Mensel and Martin Nedev (20) (Broadcast). https://tinyurl.com/mr2wpuku

Crawford, A. J., & Plavin-Masterman, M. (2025b, March 12). We have the skills, we need the connection | A conversation with Ari Luis Halos and Charnylle Antiporda (21) (Broadcast). https://tinyurl.com/bp579zfw

Crawford, A. J., & Plavin-Masterman, M. (2025c, March 26). Unlocking potential through experiential learning | A conversation with Tomás Mora and Wei Jou Huang (22) (Broadcast). https://tinyurl.com/yztxmthj

Crawford, A. J., & Plavin-Masterman, M. (2025d, June 4). Diseconomies of scale | A conversation with Michael Shuman (24) (Broadcast). https://tinyurl.com/yzxfatdp

Crawford, A., Plavin-Masterman, M., & Palmer, B. (2023, November 17). Democratize innovation. *Climate and Capital Media*. https://tinyurl.com/mtknrnbz

Crawford, A., Plavin-Masterman, M., & Palmer, B. (2024, January 19). To solve the climate crisis, go global – and bottom up. *Climate and Capital Media*. https://tinyurl.com/5n94yecx

Crippa, M., Guizzardi, D., Pagani, F., Banja, M., Muntean, M., Schaaf, E., Becker, W., Monforti-Ferrari, F., Quadrelli, R., Risquez Martin, A., Taghavi-Moharamli, P., Köykkä, J., Grassi, G., Rossi, s., Brandao De Melo, J., Oom, d., Branco, A., San-Miguel, J., & Vignati, E. (2023). *GHG emissions of all world countries*. Publications Office of the European Union. https://tinyurl.com/mrxmusas

Crunchbase. (2020). *Crunchbase diversity spotlight 2020: Funding to Black & Latinx Founders*. Crunchbase.

Cushing, E. (2021, June 22). Cancel Amazon Prime. *The Atlantic*. https://tinyurl.com/2x9s3vhx

Dartmouth Engineering (Director). (2024, June 19). AI everywhere: Transforming our world, empowering humanity. Video recording. https://tinyurl.com/36y8prze

d'Entremont, P. (2023, September 27). *Quoting you*. https://tinyurl.com/48fybzc9

digitalundivided. (2023, March 8). *Digitalundivided releases project Diane 2022 report Exploring the experiences of Latina and Black women entrepreneurs in the tech and innovation space*. https://tinyurl.com/m3c3nazk

Doughnut Economics Action Lab. (n.d.). *About doughnut economics*. https://tinyurl.com/4dpcvx2y. Accessed on February 4, 2025.

Douthat, R. (2019, June 13). Death to the meritocracy with Andrew Yang. Audio recording. https://tinyurl.com/5bux7fxk

Duncan, R. D. (2022, November 1). Results: How to get good stuff done even with disagreement in the air. *Forbes*. https://tinyurl.com/46nuwnsx

Edwards, E. (2021, February 25). Check your stats: The lack of diversity in venture capital is worse than it looks. *Forbes*. https://tinyurl.com/5fkd5wus

Ernst and Young. (2024). Tracking venture capital deployment and deal trends over time. https://tinyurl.com/2jeu5mv5. Accessed onm September 1, 2024.

Evans, R. (2023, May 9). *Part one: Jack Welch is why you got laid off*. Apple Podcasts. https://tinyurl.com/3emfzan7

Fatemi, F. (2019, March 19). *The value of investing in female founders*. https://tinyurl.com/5fpj6ct6. Accessed on January 25, 2025.

FE News, E. (2024, February 15). These states have the best school systems in the US, according to new data. *FE News*. https://tinyurl.com/mr3vpmwf

Florida, R. (2003). Cities and the creative class. *City & Community*, *2*(1).

Florida, R. (2016, February 23). *The spiky geography of venture capital in the U.S.* Bloomberg.com. https://tinyurl.com/26ckwrdp

Florida, R. (2016, January 26). The global cities where tech venture capital is concentrated. *The Atlantic Monthly*. https://tinyurl.com/mskcypux

Flynn, C. (2021). The people's climate vote. https://tinyurl.com/5avcusfs

Forrester Research. (2024). Applications of AI in health and life sciences (forrester opportunity snapshot: A custom study commissioned by SalesForce). https://tinyurl.com/2cu2smjx

Forster, E. M. (1956). *Aspects of the novel* (1st ed.). Mariner Books.

Foulk, T. A., Lanaj, K., Tu, M.-H., Erez, A., & Archambeau, L. (2018). Heavy is the head that wears the crown: An actor-centric approach to daily psychological power, abusive leader behavior, and perceived incivility. *Academy of Management Journal*, *61*(2), 661–684. https://doi.org/10.5465/amj.2015.1061

Frank, R. (2024, March 28). The wealth of the 1% just hit a record $44 trillion. *CNBC*. https://tinyurl.com/bdxk5xkr

Friedman, M. (1970, September 13). A Friedman doctrine – The social responsibility of business is to increase its profits. *The New York Times*. https://tinyurl.com/yth38jpa

Ganti, A. (July 16, 2024). How McDonald's makes money. Blog: *Investopedia*. https://tinyurl.com/yckcvxr7

Garofalo, P. (2024, July 9). When McKinsey comes to your hospital. *Boondoggle*. https://tinyurl.com/3uxcwfdx. Accessed on July 17, 2024.

Garofalo, P. (2024, June 5). Holiday travel is plagued by corporate power. *Boondoggle*. https://tinyurl.com/233369tm

Gelles, D. (2022a). *The man who broke capitalism: How Jack Welch gutted the heartland and crushed the soul of corporate America—and how to undo his legacy.* Simon & Schuster.

Gelles, D. (2022b, May 30). *What Jack Welch got wrong (just about everything).* LinkedIn. https://tinyurl.com/t7r8sydw

Gelles, D. (2024, August 1). This scientist has a risky plan to cool Earth. There's growing interest. *The New York Times*. https://tinyurl.com/8t94euwh

Georgieva, K. (2024, January 14). *AI will transform the global economy. Let's make sure it benefits humanity.* IMF. https://tinyurl.com/5n99u9bp

Ghaffary, S. (2019, September 10). Rent the runway CEO Jennifer Hyman says she has to justify her company's "right to exist" to male investors. *Vox*. https://tinyurl.com/2vnwdh4r

Ghaffary, S. (2019, September 9). The RealReal isn't buying a department store anytime soon, CEO Julie Wainwright says. *Vox*. https://tinyurl.com/us3rnk67

Gibbs, S. (2024, January 27). Google buys UK artificial intelligence startup Deepmind for £400m. *The Guardian*. https://tinyurl.com/28srk7zh

Gliadkovskaya, A. (2024). Some doctors are using ChatGPT to assist with clinical decisions. Is it safe? Fierce Health Care. https://tinyurl.com/jj4nbjv3

GLISA. (n.d.). *Small Grants Program.* https://tinyurl.com/47r8aas4. Accessed on November 21, 2024.

Global Entrepreneurship Monitor. (2024). *Economic development level.* https://tinyurl.com/sr98m7t4. Accessed on December 26, 2024.

Gomes, S. A. (2025, January 3). *From waste to resource* (Personal communication).

Gompers, P., Gornall, W., Kaplan, S. N., & Strebulaev, I. A. (2021, March 1). How venture capitalists make decisions. *Harvard Business Review*. https://tinyurl.com/3evvcy7c

Govindarajan, V., & Trimble, C. (2012). *Applying reverse innovation to make value-based care delivery work.* Harvard Business Review Press. https://tinyurl.com/3e3k5nzh. Accessed on April 20, 2024.

Grabow, J. (2024, October 24). AI continues to drive venture capital activity. *EY Insights*. https://tinyurl.com/4x7rsvde

Griffith, E., & Metz, C. (2024, August 8). The new A.I. deal: Buy everything but the company. *The New York Times*. https://tinyurl.com/35jrt55f

Gupta, V. K., & Bhawe, N. M. (2007). The influence of proactive personality and stereotype threat on women's entrepreneurial intentions. *Journal of Leadership & Organizational Studies, 13*(4), 73.

Haidt, J. (2024, March 13). End the phone-based childhood now. *The Atlantic*. https://tinyurl.com/v7fe4w35

Hansson, S., Orru, K., Siibak, A., Bäck, A., Krüger, M., Gabel, F., & Morsut, C. (2020). Communication-related vulnerability to disasters: A heuristic framework. *International Journal of Disaster Risk Reduction, 51*. https://doi.org/10.1016/j.ijdrr.2020.101931

Harder, A. (2021, April 5). Climate change action during uneven recovery risks leaving low-income people behind. *Axios*. https://tinyurl.com/nhjmfy4w

Harper, T. A. (2024). The big AI risk not enough people are seeing. *The Atlantic*. https://tinyurl.com/bdfxne9j. Accessed on May 21, 2024.

Hauer, M. E., Jacobs, S. A., & Kulp, S. A. (2024). Climate migration amplifies demographic change and population aging. *Proceedings of the National Academy of Sciences, 121*(3), e2206192119. https://doi.org/10.1073/pnas.2206192119

Haynes, T. (2018, May 1). Dopamine, smartphones & you: A battle for your time. https://tinyurl.com/5dezems7

Heffernan, M. (2015, June 16). Why it's time to forget the pecking order at work. Video recording. https://tinyurl.com/ybz35t7j

Henry, T. A. (2023). 74% of physicians work in practices that offer telehealth. https://tinyurl.com/5cmrf3as

Hill, A. (2024, November 19). 'We were horrified': Parents heartbroken as baby girl registered as male. *The Guardian*. https://tinyurl.com/44xbcr3d

Ho, W. K. (2022, July 14). The looming threat of sea level rise in Bangladesh. https://tinyurl.com/3c6f7vw5

Hoffman, R. (2023). AI field notes: OpenAI CEO Sam Altman on learnings from GPT-4 and 'impromptu' (4/3/2023). Broadcast. https://tinyurl.com/3kkhnv68. Accessed on June 29, 2024.

Hoffman, R. (2023). I wrote a book with GPT-4. Online post. LinkedIn. https://tinyurl.com/yksem6nm

Hoffman, B. (2024, February 19). Affect heuristic: What it is and how to avoid it. *Forbes*. https://tinyurl.com/4rjachh6

Hofstadter, D. (2023, July 8). Gödel, Escher, Bach, and AI. *The Atlantic*. https://tinyurl.com/yc72nmdf

Hunt, D. V., Dixon-Fyle, S., Huber, C., del Mar Martínez, M., Prince, S., & Thomas, A. (2023). *Why diversity matters even more* (pp. 1–52). McKinsey Global Institute. https://tinyurl.com/yrmvux3d

IBIS World. (2024). Global Management Consultants—Market size, industry analysis, trends and forecasts (2024–2029). https://tinyurl.com/yc57c2d7. Accessed on July 17, 2024.

ICLEI Europe. Action fund. https://tinyurl.com/5n82n8j8. Accessed on February 15, 2025.

IDMC - Internal Displacement Monitoring Centre. (2024, May 14). *2024 global report on internal displacement (GRID)*. https://tinyurl.com/bdhnymm3

International Chamber of Commerce. (2024). *The economic cost of extreme weather events*. International Chamber of Commerce. https://tinyurl.com/59d75ket

IPCC. (2022). *Climate change 2022 synthesis report, summary for policymakers*. Intergovernmental Panel on Climate Change. https://tinyurl.com/4k5byxtw

IPCC. (2023). *IPCC sixth assessment report impacts, adaptation and vulnerability summary for policymakers*. https://tinyurl.com/3b7ujh2p

Isaac, M., & Griffith, E. (2024, September 27). OpenAI is growing fast and burning through piles of money. *The New York Times*. https://tinyurl.com/4xu9k26c

Jackson, F. (2024, May 13). Banks back fossil fuels with $6.9 trillion. *Forbes*. https://tinyurl.com/yxm63f8t

Jacobs, J. (1985). *Cities and the wealth of nations: Principles of economic life*. Random House.

Jamous, L. (2024). Comments by Laudie Jamous via Zoom. Video recording. https://tinyurl.com/bdf95af8

Jensen, M., & Meckling, W. (1976). Theory of the firm: Managerial behavior, agency costs, and ownership structure. *Journal of Financial Economics*, *3*(4), 305–360.

Jordan, R. (2021, June 2). *How does climate change affect migration?* Online post. Stanford Doerr School of Sustainability. https://tinyurl.com/3r4vmwka

Küllői, P. (2019, November 27). *Towards collaborative practice - keynote 2019*.

Kanze, D., Huang, L., Conley, M. A., & Higgins, E. T. (2017, June 27). Male and female entrepreneurs get asked different questions by VCs—And it affects how much funding they get. *Harvard Business Review*. https://tinyurl.com/3pv298dd

Karim, N. (2021, April 28). Migration to flee rising seas could affect 1.3 million Bangladeshis by 2050. *Reuters*. https://tinyurl.com/mrypk4hj

Kerby, R. (2018, July 30). Where did you go to school? *The Medium*. https://tinyurl.com/4m24z36m

Khan, L. M. (2025, February 2). Stop worshiping the American tech giants. *The New York Times*. https://tinyurl.com/3mkanp8z

Kinder, M. (2024). Hollywood writers went on strike to protect their livelihoods from generative AI. Their remarkable victory matters for all workers. *Brookings*. https://tinyurl.com/2nttwwfw

King, A. (1993). From sage on the stage to guide on the side. *College Teaching*, *41*(1), 30–35.

Kolbert, E. (2024, December 14). The international court of justice takes on climate change. *The New Yorker*. https://tinyurl.com/2h4kh6rc

Kotz, M., Levermann, A., & Wenz, L. (2024). The economic commitment of climate change. *Nature*, *628*(8008). Article 8008. https://doi.org/10.1038/s41586-024-07219-0

Kreidler, M. (2024, June 17). CEO compensation skyrockets while workers' pay barely keeps up. *Capital and Main*. https://tinyurl.com/khpex242

Krskova, H., & Breyer, Y. A. (2023). The influence of growth mindset, discipline, flow and creativity on innovation: Introducing the M.D.F.C. model of innovation. *Heliyon*, *9*(3). https://doi.org/10.1016/j.heliyon.2023.e13884

Lake Superior State University (LSSU). (2016). *LSSU unleashes 42nd annual list of banished words into a post-truth world*. 2017 Banished Words List. https://tinyurl.com/4auxncud. Accessed on January 1, 2025.

Lala, C., & Palladino, L. (2020). *Shareholders first: What hasn't changed since the business roundtable's 2019 statement*. Roosevelt Institute. https://tinyurl.com/4b6ys4vj

Lewis, M. (2004). *Moneyball: The art of winning an unfair game: (First)*. W. W. Norton & Company. https://tinyurl.com/5f8jzwkr

Lovins, H. (2025, January 24). As LA fires still burn, how can we rebuild? *Climate and Capital*. https://tinyurl.com/muwvp7nt

Lunden, I. (2024, October 29). LinkedIn launches its first AI agent to take on the role of job recruiters. *TechCrunch*. https://tinyurl.com/y95u9ksx

Lynn, J. (1992). *My cousin vinnie*. Video recording.

Macrotrends. (2024). Alphabet gross profit 2010–2023 | GOOG. *Macrotrends*. https://tinyurl.com/3dswjw2j

Maitland, A., Lawson, M., Stroot, H., Poidatz, A., Khalfan, A., & Dabi, N. (2022). Carbon billionaires: The investment emissions of the world's richest people. https://tinyurl.com/yhjdtvdc

Majic Predin, J. (2024, July 25). The resurgence of crypto VC investing: Navigating the new bull run. *Forbes*. https://tinyurl.com/yt29dx3y

Malito, A. (2017). Women are about to control a massive amount of wealth but can't find anyone to manage it. *Market Watch*. https://tinyurl.com/mr2d9av3. Accessed on July 11, 2024.

Mangelsdorf, M. E. (2017, December 11). The trouble with homogeneous teams. *MIT Sloan Management Review*. https://tinyurl.com/4t28abrp

Mann, J., & Kay, G. (2024, January 11). Google just laid off hundreds of staff. Read the email notifying some workers. *Business Insider*. https://tinyurl.com/4x3bhzv7

Manyika, J., Birshan, M., Smit, S., Woetzel, J., Russell, K., Purcell, L., & Ramaswamy, S. (2021). *A new look at how corporations impact the economy and households*. McKinsey Global Institute.

Mascarenhas, N. (2020, August 5). The story behind Rent the Runway's first check. *TechCrunch*. https://tinyurl.com/3sxrftpm

Massachusetts Middle School Teacher. (January 2, 2025). *The makerspace and the junk corner*.

Mazzucato, M., & Collington, R. (2023). *The big con: How the consulting industry weakens our businesses, infantilizes our governments and warps our economies*. Penguin Press.

McAllister, S. (2024, October 23). There could be 1.2 billion climate refugees by 2050. Here's what you need to know. *Zurich Magazine*. https://tinyurl.com/4y5jmfcz

McCann, A. (2024, July 22). States with the best & worst school systems in 2025. WalletHub. https://wallethub.com/edu/e/states-with-the-best-schools/5335

McKinsey. (2023). The state of AI in 2023: Generative AI's breakout year. *McKinsey*. https://tinyurl.com/223wy2d6

Medintz, S. (2024, April 16). Climate change could cost each American born today $500,000. *Consumer Reports*. https://tinyurl.com/yzeuwaa9

Menczer, F. (2021, October 7). Here's exactly how social media algorithms can manipulate you. *Big Think*. https://tinyurl.com/mrx6tstz

Meta Investor Relations. (2025, January 29). *Meta reports fourth quarter and full year 2024 results*. https://tinyurl.com/28za53tu

Metcalfe, T. (2024, January 26). The Roman Empire's worst plagues were linked to climate change. *Scientific American*. https://tinyurl.com/mu5rz97e

Metinko, C. (2024, January 9). Artificial buildup: AI startups were hot in 2023, but this year may be slightly different. *Crunchbase News*. https://tinyurl.com/4xytvpmd

Mitchell, S. (December 1, 2024). *The great grocery squeeze*. https://tinyurl.com/bd2p9mtd

Morin, E., & Kern, A. B. (1999). *Homeland Earth: A manifesto for the new millennium*. https://tinyurl.com/2tywcm2p

Morris, L. (2023, April 18). 46% of practices are already using Chatbots to assess patient symptoms, and that number is going to go up. https://tinyurl.com/4tewkuur

Morris, C., Grauerholz-Fisher, E., Ellsworth, M. E., & Crocker, C. E. (2024). A primer on private equity ownership in ABA. *Behavior Analysis in Practice.* https://doi.org/10.1007/s40617-024-00941-1

Moses, C., & Suhartono, M. (2024, May 21). One dead and dozens injured after 'extreme turbulence' on flight. https://tinyurl.com/yujer6ua

Muis, Q., & Reeskens, T. (2021). Are we in this together? Changes in anti-immigrant sentiments during the COVID-19 pandemic. *International Journal of Intercultural Relations, 86.* https://doi.org/10.1016/j.ijintrel.2021.12.006

Murphy, M. (2024). *Cultures of growth.* Simon & Schuster.

Musharbash, B. (2025, January 25). Did a private equity fire truck roll-up worsen the L.A. fires? *BIG by Matt Stoller.* https://tinyurl.com/3j9svb9t

News Wires. (2023, July 11). *McKinsey & Company pushes fossil fuel interests as advisor to UN climate talks, whistleblowers say.* France 24. https://tinyurl.com/2ujtm4zy

Nicholson, S. (2020, September 30). Solar radiation management. *Wilson Center Environmental Change and Security Program.* https://tinyurl.com/bdhre4zt

Niranjan, A. (2024, July 23). Sunday was world's hottest ever recorded day, data suggests. *The Guardian.* https://tinyurl.com/23pbyuer

Nisbett, R. E., & Wilson, T. D. (1977). The halo effect: Evidence for unconscious alteration of judgments. *Journal of Personality and Social Psychology, 35*(4), 250–256.

Noah, T., Medina, C. M. & Johnson, J. (2024, December 12). What now? With Trevor Noah. *Apple Podcasts.* https://tinyurl.com/yd5kmxv9

Nocera, J., & McLean, B. (2023, October 28). What financial engineering does to hospitals. *The Atlantic.* https://tinyurl.com/2bzsj9vy

Noland, M., & Moran, T. (2016, February 8). Study: Firms with more women in the C-suite are more profitable. *Harvard Business Review.* https://tinyurl.com/59tnfdj7

Notopoulos, K. (2024, May). Google AI said to put glue in pizza—So I made a pizza with glue and ate it. *Business Insider.* https://tinyurl.com/28782zcu

Novak, M. (2024, June 13). Elon Musk says optimus robot will "babysit your kids" in weirdest prediction yet. *Gizmodo.* https://tinyurl.com/ktrhh6y5

NRDC. (2018, September 13). Bangladesh: A country underwater, a culture on the move. https://tinyurl.com/4av8s4yj

O'Connor, G. (2004). *Miracle (2004)—IMDb.* Video recording. https://tinyurl.com/5e2bmpad

O'Neill, K. (2024, January 18). *Interview by Alejandro Crawford* [Video Interview with Dr. O'Neill in Baghdad].

OECD. (2016). *OECD entrepreneurship at a glance 2016.* OECD Publishing. https://tinyurl.com/3sv38bzr

Okereke, C. (2023, April 18). Opinion | My continent is not your giant climate laboratory (Published 2023). *The New York Times.* https://tinyurl.com/24u4a4mb

Oxfam. (2023, November 20). Top 5 ways billionaires are driving climate change. https://tinyurl.com/yem8pwnh

Paddison, L. (2021, October 27). How the rich are driving climate change. *BBC.* https://tinyurl.com/42bu4fbh

Page, B. I., Bartels, L. M., & Seawright, J. (2013). Democracy and the policy preferences of wealthy Americans. *Perspectives on Politics, 11*(1), 51–73. https://doi.org/10.1017/S153759271200360X

Palladino, L. (2019). *Ending shareholder primacy in corporate governance.* Roosevelt Institute. https://tinyurl.com/3wkwwea9

Panons, J. (2024, July 13). Surrey: Action fund launched to help tackle climate change. *BBC.* https://tinyurl.com/596dsnwe

Parisot, D. (Director). (1999, December 25). *Galaxy Quest* (Adventure, Comedy, Sci-Fi). Dreamworks Pictures, Gran Via Productions.

Patil, S. A. (2023). Private equity in ophthalmology and optometry: A time series analysis from 2012 to 2021. https://tinyurl.com/vruf6fdx

Paul, R., & Varadhan, S. (2023, April 20). Bangladesh suffers widespread power outages during relentless heat. *Reuters.* https://tinyurl.com/ybh33es8

Pink, D. (2011). *Drive: The surprising truth about what motivates us.* Riverhead Books (PenguinRandomHouse). https://tinyurl.com/2hcdtz9u

Pod Save America (Director). (2023, March 30). Donald Trump indicted by Grand Jury, would become first president charged with a crime. Video recording. https://tinyurl.com/yv59vrem

Poetz, M., Franke, N., & Schreier, M. (2014, November 21). Sometimes the best ideas come from outside your industry. *Harvard Business Review.* https://tinyurl.com/5fav82kb

Popper, K. R. (1994). *The open society and its enemies* (Kindle Edition). Princeton University Press.

Porter, E. (2019, February 4). Tech is splitting the U.S. Work Force in two. *The New York Times.* https://tinyurl.com/4a8txtym

Potter, E. [@drelisabethpotter]. (2025, February 3). UnitedHealthcare's response: Read it for yourself [Image]. Instagram. https://tinyurl.com/y4a8f3bx

Potter, E. [@drelisabethpotter]. (2025, January 8). It's 2025 and insurance just keeps getting worse [Video]. Instagram. https://tinyurl.com/yc28hxtc

Poushter, J., Fagan, M., & Gubbala, S. (2022). Climate change remains top global threat across 19-country survey. https://tinyurl.com/mwnerwue

Private Equity Stakeholder Project. (2024). PESP private equity hospital tracker. https://tinyurl.com/mpp3n84m

Procopio, J. (2024, November 5). LinkedIn's hostile takeover of the tech job market: LinkedIn is going all-in on AI for recruiters and job seekers. Inc. https://tinyurl.com/5dyjmnzp

Pulcrano, J., Boyman, O., Schmedders, K., & Werner, M. U. (2024). Why diversification could be a winning formula for VC funds. https://tinyurl.com/43sbwna6

Pulliam, S., & Mullins, B. (2017, December 29). The modern campaign-finance loophole: Governors associations. *Wall Street Journal.* https://tinyurl.com/2s3t4mv9

PYMNTS. (2024, December 16). AI companies receive 42% of US venture capital investment. https://tinyurl.com/2ejyvcx2

Raikes, J. (2024, March 22). Murphy's law: How 'cultures of genius' Hinder competitiveness. *Forbes.* https://tinyurl.com/4r2xbtph

Reich, R. (2024, November 8). The real lesson we should draw from what occurred Tuesday. *Substack.* https://robertreich.substack.com/

Reich, R. (2024, September 24). Buying back chips. *Substack.* https://robertreich.substack.com/

Rettner, R. (2010, May 2). Apple obsession: The science of iPad fanaticism. *Live Science*. https://tinyurl.com/4u7jtbpx

Ripple, W., & Wolf, C. (2024, January 9). Scientists outline a bold solution to climate change, biodiversity loss, social injustice. https://tinyurl.com/2ynbbtp9

Ritchie, H. (2024, April 8). What share of global CO_2 emissions come from aviation? *Our World in Data*. https://tinyurl.com/m94yvtwe

Ritchie, H., Rosado, P., & Roser, M. (2020). *Breakdown of carbon dioxide, methane and nitrous oxide emissions by sector*. Dataset. OurWorldInData.org. https://tinyurl.com/4br5m3xu

Robbins, J. (2024, December 24). Nearly 1 in 4 new startups is an AI company. *Pitchbook*. https://tinyurl.com/54mmfcwj

Roberts, M. (2023, March 1). *The big con*. https://tinyurl.com/5bpz43x5

Robinson, K. (2008, June 16). *Changing education paradigms*. Transcript. https://tinyurl.com/5cvujdxs

Robinson, N. (2023, February 10). Exposing the secretive and sinister work of McKinsey & Co. *Current Affairs*. https://tinyurl.com/2hm2dhns

Roman, P. (1981, April 28). The peanuts classics. Broadcast. In *It's magic, Charlie Brown*. https://tinyurl.com/ytpjczhc

Roose, K. (2024, May 10). Meet Kevin's AI friends (82). Broadcast. https://tinyurl.com/yc5hm6f5. Accessed on May 26, 2024.

Roose, K. (2025, January 28). Why DeepSeek could change what Silicon Valley believes about A.I. *The New York Times*. https://tinyurl.com/2s3zyrwu

Sahebi, H., Khodoomi, M., Seif, M., Pishvaee, M., & Hanne, T. (2023). The benefits of peer-to-peer renewable energy trading and battery storage backup for local grid. *Journal of Energy Storage*. https://tinyurl.com/36372uby

Samuelson, J. (2022, March 16). *The impact of shareholder primacy: What it means to put the stock price first*. The Aspen Institute. https://tinyurl.com/5ekpskzz

Sanders, H. (2024, June 21). 260 McNuggets? McDonald's ends A.I. drive-through tests amid errors. *The New York Times*. https://tinyurl.com/3v66tjkk

Santa Clara Valley Historical Society. (1994a). *Steve Jobs secrets of life*. Video recording. https://tinyurl.com/mw6rfk8v

Santa Clara Valley Historical Society. (1994b). *Steve Jobs secrets of life*. Video recording. https://tinyurl.com/3ja4vcz3

Sarasvathy, S. (2008). What makes entrepreneurs entrepreneurial. *SSRN Electronic Journal*. https://doi.org/10.2139/ssrn.909038; https://tinyurl.com/j5pfhck4

Sarlin, J. (2024, June 21). TikTok pulls new AI tool that spouted Hitler on command, horrified experts. Video recording. *CNN Business*. https://tinyurl.com/34fdynwv

Scheffler, R. A., Alexander, L., Fulton, B., Arnold, D., & Abdelhadi, O. A. (2023). *Monetizing medicine: Private equity and competition in physician practice markets*. American Antitrust Institute. https://tinyurl.com/2ubbsnd3

Schumpeter, J. (1942). *Capitalism, socialism, and democracy*. Harper and Brothers.

Schwerin, M. (2022, May 29). Airlines' premium-economy trick. *The Atlantic*. https://tinyurl.com/3wucvy55

SEI. (2023). *The production gap: Phasing down or phasing up? Top fossil fuel producers plan even more extraction despite climate promises*. Stockholm Environment Institute (SEI), Climate Analytics, E3G, International Institute for Sustainable Development (IISD). https://tinyurl.com/3mz8h3e4

Shawbel, D. (2011, October 26). Gallup's Jim Clifton on the coming jobs war. *Forbes.* https://tinyurl.com/mr2vnh24

Shraiman, A. (2024). *Banking on climate chaos: Fossil fuel finance report 2024.* https://tinyurl.com/ys8kjyup

Shuman, M. (2023, July 17). *Reflections from May 1–3, 2023, visit to South Australia (Memo to Green Industries SA).*

Shuman, M. (2024, October 10). Great news! Venture capital is having a bad year. Substack. *The Main Street Journal.* https://tinyurl.com/4y5udmtu

Simon, J. (2024, April 21). *Startups want to cool Earth by reflecting sunlight. There are few rules and big risks.* NPR. https://tinyurl.com/54b47vxr

Singh, Y., Song, Z., Polsky, D., Bruch, J. D., & Zhu, J. M. (2022). Association of private equity acquisition of physician practices with changes in health care spending and utilization. *JAMA Health Forum, 3*(9), e222886. https://tinyurl.com/354aex9k

Smialek, J. (2024, July 3). America's divided summer economy is coming to an airport or hotel near you. *The New York Times.* https://tinyurl.com/3k92khmp

Smith, B. L. (2023). How to see the invisible. https://tinyurl.com/23jdmbh4

Smith, B. L. (2024, April 18). *A Google Search in service of life.* Substack. Matereal World. https://tinyurl.com/cpffazp

Sofge, E. (2010, April 8). A history of Iron men: Top 5 iconic exoskeletons. *Popular Mechanics.* https://tinyurl.com/mpvuzpyx

Sohail, M. (2024, April 7). The availability heuristic: Cognitive bias in decision making. *The Psychology Square.* https://tinyurl.com/4su8uc9b

Solar Geoengineering Non-Use Agreement. (2022, January). *Solar Geoengineering Non-Use Agreement.* https://www.solargeoeng.org/

Stanford Graduate School of Business (Director). (2014, March 8). Marc Andreessen on big breakthrough ideas and courageous entrepreneurs. Video recording. https://tinyurl.com/th7eb98v

Starkey, K., & Tempest, S. (January 13, 2025). The business school and the end of history: Reimagining management education. *The Academy of Management Learning and Education.* https://doi.org/10.5465/amle.2024.0033

Statista. (2024, April). Internet and social media users in the world in 2024. *Statista.* https://tinyurl.com/34shuymw

Steinmann, J., Pieters, L., Cascone, J., Pankratz, D. M., & Novak, D. R. (2025, January 14). Sustainability has staying power. *Deloitte Center for Integrated Research.* https://tinyurl.com/2s3t3xa9

Stout, L. (2012). The problem of corporate purpose. *Issues in Governance Studies, 48,* 14. https://tinyurl.com/5fs8bd7a

Surowiecki, J. (2024, January 15). What's gone wrong at Boeing. *The Atlantic.* https://tinyurl.com/bdhhh6th

Taleb, N. N. (2013). *Antifragile* (Kindle Edition). Penguin Books. https://tinyurl.com/yj53d7p6

Teare, G. (2023, April 5). Global VC funding falls dramatically across all stages in rocky Q1, despite massive OpenAI and Stripe deals. *Crunchbase News.* https://tinyurl.com/2s4b4ehr

Teirstein, Z. (2024, October 22). The flood that forced a housing reckoning in Vermont. *The Grist.* https://tinyurl.com/5sc2c277

The World's Most Polluting Industries. (2023, May 11). *Climate Change News*. https://tinyurl.com/43s6yyh3

Thorbecke, C. (2024, January 13). The tech sector is pouring billions of dollars into AI. But it keeps laying off humans. *CNN Business*. https://tinyurl.com/y4k3md6t

UN World Food Programme (WFP). (2021). UN World Food Programme (WFP). https://tinyurl.com/3nats6sd

UNFCCC. (2023). COP28 joint statement on climate, nature and people. https://tinyurl.com/2b6r4wyv

Valentine, S. (2024, July 18). How cleaning up shipping cut pollution—And warmed the planet. *Grist*. https://tinyurl.com/3xk67tuz

Varanasi, L. (2023, November 5). GPT-4 can ace the bar, but it only has a decent chance of passing the CFA exams. Here's a list of difficult exams the ChatGPT and GPT-4 have passed. *Business Insider*. https://tinyurl.com/ymwv7d2r

Vedantam, S. (2021). *How they see us*. Audio recording. https://tinyurl.com/3r6n2smn. Accessed on October 11, 2024.

Velez, D. O. (2024, April 4). Caribbean matters: Guyanese president spars with BBC host, goes viral. *Daily Kos*. https://tinyurl.com/4wwj3skb

Vetter, D. (2022, January 20). Solar geoengineering: Why Bill Gates wants it, but these experts want to stop it. *Forbes*. https://tinyurl.com/5cmjkk7a

Vipond, T. (2014). *How VCs look at startups and founders*. Corporate Finance Institute. https://tinyurl.com/yuu2sf5e

Washington State Department of Commerce. (2024, November 12). *Climate planning grants*. https://tinyurl.com/4t8472vu

Weber, L. (2022, September 19). *Private equity sees the billions in eye care as firms target high-profit procedures*. KFF Health News. https://tinyurl.com/48eankbu

Weider, B. (2014, May 8). Big money comes to state attorney-general races. *The Atlantic*. https://tinyurl.com/y7c7x93b

Weil, E. (2023). Sam Altman is the Oppenheimer of our age: OpenAI's CEO thinks he knows our future. What do we know about him? *The New York Times Magazine*. https://tinyurl.com/mpzytte4. Accessed June 29, 2024

Whiting, K. (2023, March 7). This is why "polycrisis" is a useful way of looking at the world right now. Online post. https://tinyurl.com/mu94s54y

Wired, I. (2024, April). How SOLshare's Sebastian Groh wants to create a wave of climate startups. *Wired*. https://tinyurl.com/4prj9fw7. Accessed December 30, 2024

World Bank. (2021, September 13). *Groundswell report*. World Bank. https://tinyurl.com/5n6znpek

World Health Organization. (2022, July 1). *New report highlights the impact of changes in the environment on one health*. https://tinyurl.com/29z92xrz

Yang, A. (2016, January 8). What's eating Silicon Valley. *Quartz*. https://tinyurl.com/26m5shd4

Zickgraf, C. (2023, October 4). Where are all the climate migrants? Explaining immobility amid environmental change. https://tinyurl.com/5h2p5fs8

Zitron, E. (2024a, April 23). The man who killed Google Search. *Ed Zitron's Where's Your Ed At*. https://tinyurl.com/yytbvf6d

Zitron, E. (2024b, June 3). The Rot-Com Bubble. *Ed Zitron's Where's Your Ed At*. https://tinyurl.com/4yen37nh

Zitron, E. (2024c, June 11). Silicon Valley's false prophet. *Ed Zitron's Where's Your Ed At*. https://tinyurl.com/4u4xmv8n

Zitron, E. (2024d, July 1). The shareholder supremacy. *Ed Zitron's Where's Your Ed At*. https://tinyurl.com/4bbtbcd9

Zitron, E. (2024e, July 24). Rot economics - An interview with MIT's Daron Acemoglu. Interview. https://shorturl.at/TrGAv

Zitron, E. (2024f, October 2). OpenAI is a bad business. *Ed Zitron's Where's Your Ed At*. https://tinyurl.com/2awupm3j

Zitron, E. (2024g, September 16). The subprime AI crisis. *Ed Zitron's Where's Your Ed At*. https://tinyurl.com/4snbtbrd

Zitron, E. (2024h, December 3). Godot isn't making it. *Ed Zitron's Where's Your Ed At*. https://tinyurl.com/yc74erpc

Zitron, E. (2025, January 29). Deep impact. *Ed Zitron's Where's Your Ed At*. https://tinyurl.com/y9xz7k88

Zonneveld, K. A., Harper, K., Klugel, A., Chen, L., De Lange, G., & Versteegh, G. J. (2024). Climate change, society, and pandemic disease in Roman Italy between 200 BCE and 600 CE. *Science Advances*, *10*(4). https://www.science.org/doi/10.1126/sciadv.adk1033

Index

www.ingramcontent.com/pod-product-compliance
Lightning Source LLC
Chambersburg PA
CBHW061252220326

41599CB00028B/5623